Louisiana

OFF THE

BEATEN

PATH™

SECOND EDITION

GAY MARTIN

A Voyager Book

The Globe Pequot Press

Old Saybrook, Connecticut

ABOUT THE AUTHOR

Gay N. Martin, who has lived in several southeastern states, now makes her home in Alabama. She has published more than 250 articles in national newspapers and magazines and especially enjoys writing about travel in the Southeast. She has won more than thirty writing awards for fiction and nonfiction.

Before she made a New Year's resolution to turn her writing hobby into a career, Mrs. Martin taught high school for eleven years, served as resource coordinator of her school's gifted program, and sponsored the school newspaper. Her work has appeared in *Modern Bride, Boston Herald, Kiwanis, The Writer, Seventeen, Atlantic Journal-Constitution, Grand Rapids Press, The London Free Press, Milwaukee Sentinel,* and other publications. She is the author of Globe Pequot's *Alabama: Off the Beaten Path.*

Mrs. Martin and her husband, a dentist, have five children.

Copyright © 1990, 1993 by Gay Martin
Cover map © DeLorme Mapping

Library of Congress Cataloging-in-Publication Data
Martin, Gay N.
    Louisiana : off the beaten path / by Gay N. Martin. — 2nd ed.
        p.   cm.
    "A Voyager book."
    Includes index.
    ISBN 1-56440-233-9
    1. Louisiana—Guidebooks.   I. Title.
F367.3.M37   1993
917.6304'63—dc20

Manufactured in the United States of America
Second Edition/Second Printing   93-1326
                                                                        CIP

CONTENTS

To my husband, Carlton,
who remains wonderful—"Here is for Papou."

ACKNOWLEDGMENTS

Many wonderful people helped with this book. I'd like to thank all who shared some of their Louisiana with me, particularly the following: Marie and Leon Standifer, Vicki and Ronald Martin, Kay and Cliff LaFrance, Nita and Larry Rogers, Anne and Frank Fitzgerald, Liz and Richard Kempe, Charles Norton, Sondra and Black Guidry, Elise Lattier and TRUTH, Sue M. Edmunds, Keith Winter, Wendell McCluer, Kathi and Bill Caldwell, Julia Trichell, Mary and T-jun Segura and family, Janie Lipscomb, Vera Erwin, Carol McGee Thomas, Preston Friedley, Jerel M. Giarrusso, Betty Reed, Dayna Johnson, Dr. Michael J. Caire, Carol Layton Parsons, Faye Russell, Cindy DePierri, Frances Leake, Kelly Strenge, Nicole Spangenberg, Cynthia Bealer, Martha Estes, Donna Boudoin, Danny Bonaventure, Joyce Benoit, Betty Jones, Roxana Benoit, Elizabeth Hardy, Clarence L. Powers, Roy C. Holleman, and former Louisiana residents, E. L. Hill and Dixie and Buddy Huthmaker.

Other friendly natives who extended a helping hand include: Patti Young, Sue Ellen Lewis, Barbara West, Judy M. Lowentritt, Beverly Gianna, Christine DeCuir, Puddy Solina, Rodney Guilbeaux, Langford Peavy, Bill Turnbull, Gregory N. Marcantel, Dr. Charles H. Gideon, Betty Stewart, Charlene Daniels, Jessica and Bart Weems, Ruth H. Cabral, Mary Lou Perkins, Dianne Jarreau, Jennifer Harsh, Becky Aleshire, Bruce Morgan, Ann Johnson, Steele Burden, Mibs Bartkiewicz, Katie S. Chiasson, Carola Ann Andrepont, Maralee Prigmore, Mary Ann Weilbaecher, Dan Fuselier, Kathy and Johnny Richard, Gerard and Joel Sellers, Flo Milsted, Gayle Q. Brown, Jennifer and Mark Seale, Andrew G. Barry, Karen McMinn, Allison Drew, Carol Costello, Johnie W. McKinney, Sybil McCann, Anne Butler, Jeffrey H. Landesberg, Joeann and Fred McLemore, Nancy Noone Broussard, Mary Moats, Marjorie Doyle, Captain Lawrence Keeton, Keith Tinnin, James McGlade, and Darrin Unruh.

Also I'm grateful to Carolyn and Bill Mason, Tom Drinkard, Wilda Eddy, Nancy Jo Hardy, Robin Cooper, and the fine folks at the Millsaps Buie House in Jackson, Mississippi.

A special thank-you goes to Lisa and Kevin Karch, who honeymooned in Louisiana and found it fascinating, and to Scott Standifer, who recommended the destination. Most of all I'd like to thank Edith Sorrells Newsom (who may be blamed for my wandering ways).

INTRODUCTION

Louisiana offers diversity with a capital *D*. The state's shape looks like a boot or perhaps a Santa Claus stocking, raveling at the toe. Both its culture and geography can be described as unique. Nowhere else in this country do you find parishes instead of counties—a carryover from the original divisions drawn by the Roman Catholic Church.

Natives tend to divide their state simply—North Louisiana and South Louisiana with New Orleans as a third entity. North and south merge at Alexandria, in the middle of the state. Actually the internal "Mason-Dixon" line can be drawn just south of Alexandria at Bayou Boeuf (called BYE-yoo BUFF by natives of French origin and BYE-yoo BEFF by other local folks).

For the purpose of clustering regional attractions, this book breaks the "boot" into five sections. Starting with the northwestern region, the text moves from west to east in zigzag fashion, culminating in the southeastern area on the doorstep of New Orleans. "The city that care forgot" would serve as a fitting finale for a Louisiana holiday, and several enticements, such as the Garden District and Vieux Carré (French Quarter), are suggested as part of a New Orleans itinerary. As the state's principal tourist magnet, New Orleans (that's pronounced "N'yawlins") hardly qualifies as being off the beaten path; however, it would be a shame to miss some of this grand city's unique attractions.

Traveling through the state I conducted a personal poll. "What's the best thing about Louisiana?" I asked almost everyone I met. Responses ranged from fishing, hunting, and history to climate and "flowers that bloom all year long," but the majority came up with two emphatic answers: "the people" and "the food." And I have to agree—both are wonderful.

"The people here are wonderful, gentle, and kind," said a man from West Monroe (who also maintains a home in New Hampshire). "They say good morning to everyone they meet, even strangers. That's what I like most about Louisiana." Both locals and transplanted citizens claimed, "You won't find better seafood anywhere else in the world." Menus feature everything from broiled, baked, boiled, blackened, steamed, and fried fish to delectable concoctions of gumbo, shrimp Creole, crabmeat crepes, crawfish bisque, *étouffée*, jambalaya, oysters Rockefeller, and pompano *en papillote*. With cuisines ranging from Acadian and Creole to Southern—well, what more can be said?

In selecting trip souvenirs consider cookbooks. In each region you'll come across excellent cookbooks featuring local specialties, not surprising in a state that takes food seriously and regards cooking an art.

Louisianians also show a fondness for festivals. Practically any topic is good enough for a celebration—possums, peaches, pecans, poke salad, pirates, sweet potatoes, frogs, catfish, rice, oil, crawfish, and the list goes on. (Incidentally, despite what your biology teacher may have told you, the proper term here is crawfish—not crayfish.) The merrymaking, which always includes good music and great food, can also feature such festivities as frog derbies, crawfish-eating contests, and pirogue races. Of course all the world knows about the state's biggest festival, Mardi Gras (French for "fat Tuesday") with its magic, music, and mystique. To enhance your visit to a particular area, find out about any nearby festivals—they fill the calendar.

The state boasts a number of the South's grand plantation manors, and many are mentioned in this guide. If you're a history buff, be sure to check the area through which you're traveling for other showplaces that may be in the same vicinity. Some historic homes, not open on a regular basis, can be visited by appointment. A great number, especially along River Road, offer year-round tours. Best of all, many of these mansions now open their doors to travelers, inviting them to sleep in canopied beds, wake up to coffee delivered on a silver platter, and enjoy a full plantation breakfast of grits, ham, eggs, and biscuits or perhaps sugared stacks of French toast with sausages.

You can also take a look at the lifestyles of early citizens who endured hardship and privation. Their customs and contributions are commemorated in museums across the state—from the Acadian Village and Homer's Ford Museum to Shreveport's Pioneer Heritage Center and Baton Rouge's Rural Life Museum.

Some general observations: North Louisiana's culture and topography resemble those of surrounding states—Mississippi, Arkansas, and Texas. This area is primarily Protestant. In contrast, most of South Louisiana's landscape features marshes, swamps, bayous, and bottomlands. Predominantly Catholic, many of its inhabitants descended from the French Acadians, who were forced by England to leave Canada in 1755. *Evangeline*, Longfellow's epic poem, tells their story. In time the pronunciation of "Acadian" was reduced to "Cajun." Known for their *joie de vivre,* or joy of life, Cajuns treasure their ancestry, and many still speak the Cajun-French language.

To promote understanding between the "two Louisianas," city representatives from Ruston, in the state's north-central region, and Opelousas, in the heart of the southern section's Acadiana, initiated an in-state cultural and educational exchange program. Ruston followed up with Jennings as a sister city in this ongoing plan that encourages high school students and city officials to spend time in other regions and fosters a mutual appreciation of the state's cultural differences. Other cities, such as Shreveport and Lafayette also participate in the swap-off.

The state's economy took a dip when gas and oil prices plummeted, but folks say it's made them look to new resources, such as tourism. Tourism now ranks as the state's second leading nonagricultural industry, and current growth projections indicate it will jump to number one by the year 2000. "With our massive road rebuilding program now in progress, Louisiana will have some of the finest highways in the country within the next few years," says Preston Friedley, president of the Shreveport-Bossier Convention and Tourist Bureau.

Wherever you enter the state, stop at the first welcome station you see and collect information on local attractions. To hold all your brochures and maps, you might be given a bag that says LOUISIANA—AS AMERICAN AS CRAWFISH PIE.

Dates, rates, times, attractions, and facilities tend to change, so please call ahead to double-check pertinent information before making a long trip to a particular place. For a free road map of the state, write: Louisiana Department of Culture, Recreation and Tourism, Office of Tourism, P.O. Box 94291, Baton Rouge, LA 70804—9291, or call 1–800–33GUMBO or (504) 342–8119. You can also request a directory of state festivals and a vacation packet tailored to your interests.

Unless otherwise noted, all museums and attractions with admission prices $5.00 or less per adult will be designated as modest. A restaurant meal (the price of a single entrée without beverages) listed as economical costs less than $7.00, moderate prices range between $7.00 and $18.00, and entrées more than $18.00 are classified as expensive. As for accommodations, those that cost less than $70.00 per night will be listed as standard, an overnight stay falling in the $70.00 to $150.00 range is labeled moderate, and lodging more than $150.00 is designated deluxe.

Louisiana possesses many wonderful, tucked-away towns and special spots—more than can be included in this volume. If this sampler whets your appetite for a statewide exploration of your own, you'll discover a smorgasbord of tempting offerings. Take along your curiosity and your appetite when you head for Louisiana and let the good times roll! Or, as they put it in Cajun country, *"Laissez les bons temps rouler!"*

The prices and rates listed in this guidebook were confirmed at press time. We recommend, however, that you call establishments before traveling to obtain current information.

NORTHWEST LOUISIANA

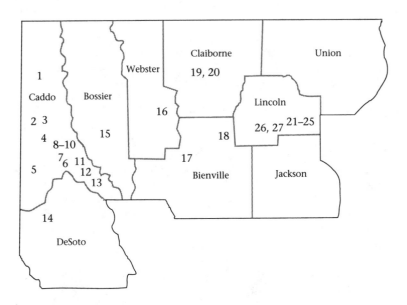

Claiborne
19, 20

Union

1

Webster

Caddo   Bossier

16

Lincoln

26, 27 21–25

2 3

15

18

4   8–10

7 11

6

5

12

13

17

Bienville

Jackson

14

DeSoto

1. Caddo-Pine Island Oil and Historical Society Museum
2. Stumpwater Inn Restaurant
3. Walter B. Jacobs Memorial Nature Park
4. Freeman and Harris Cafe
5. American Rose Center
6. Grass Roots Country Cottage
7. Fairfield Place
8. Spring Street Museum
9. The Blind Tiger
10. Strand Theatre
11. Meadows Museum of Art
12. Pioneer Heritage Center
13. Dudley and Gerald's South Louisiana Kitchen
14. Keatchie

15. Touchstone Wildlife and Art Museum
16. Germantown Colony Museum
17. Bonnie and Clyde Ambush Site
18. Bienville Depot Museum
19. Ford Museum
20. Claiborne Parish Courthouse
21. Lincoln Parish Museum
22. Dixie Theater
23. Piney Hills Gallery
24. Erma's
25. Log Cabin Smokehouse
26. Idea Place
27. Bee's Cafe

NORTHWEST LOUISIANA

CADDO PARISH

Entering Louisiana at its northwest corner, a person can stand in three states at the same time. North of Rodessa the Three States Marker shows where the borders of Louisiana, Texas, and Arkansas all converge. Shreveport and Bossier City, farther south, serve as the hub for a 200-mile radius known as the **Ark-La-Tex.** The Shreveport-Bossier area makes a convenient starting point for exploring other portions of Louisiana. From here you can either proceed eastward across the top of the boot, or you can angle south into the central section. Both regions provide plenty of off-the-beaten-path attractions.

Named for the Native Americans who once lived here, Caddo Parish was created in 1838. The Caddo (or Kadohadacho) Native Americans who occupied the surrounding forests sold one million acres to the United States government on July 1, 1835.

Afterward, with the discovery of oil, the area turned from happy hunting grounds to hootin' and hollerin' hysteria almost overnight. In one year land values jumped from 50 cents an acre to $500 an acre. Oil City sprang up to become the first wildcat town in the Ark-La-Tex. The resulting large red-light district and influx of rough characters gave the town an unsavory reputation.

When you enter today's Oil City via Route 1 from the state's northwestern corner, you'll find a small, quiet hamlet with few reminders of its brawling boomtown days. One clue is Discovery Well, an exact replica of the area's first oil well, drilled here in 1906. Located about two blocks off Route 1, this derrick stands near the ✦ **Caddo-Pine Island Oil and Historical Society Museum** at 207 Land Avenue (Oil City's main street). Presently the complex consists of three buildings dating from the early 1900s plus a museum now under construction.

Start your tour at the museum, housed in the town's old railroad depot, which was donated by Kansas City Southern Railroad. You'll see displays of early oil field equipment, railroad artifacts, old photographs, Native American relics, a collection of pearls found in mussels from Caddo Lake, and other items relating to the area's history.

A fifteen-minute video presentation acquaints you with North Caddo Parish's history, and your guide will share some of the region's colorful legends, such as the story of an Indian chief who divided his extensive land holdings between his twin sons. Each brave was told to walk for two and a half days—one toward the rising sun and the other toward the setting sun. The east-ward-bound son received Louisiana's Natchitoches area as his legacy, and the other's inheritance was the region around Nacog-doches, Texas.

The museum, which closes for lunch from noon to 1:00 P.M., is open Monday through Friday from 9:00 A.M. until 5:00 P.M. and on Saturday by appointment only. Admission is modest. Call (318) 995–6845.

After touring the museum, step across the street to see the turn-of-the-century bank and post office (which was moved from nearby Trees City); both are enclosed by a chain-link fence. A security system now protects the small bank, although none was there when the bank did a booming cash business.

Perhaps the closest Oil City comes to its lively past occurs each spring when citizens celebrate the oil industry with their Gusher Days Festival. On tap are such events as arts-and-crafts exhibits, street dancing, parades, and a beard contest. Previous festivals featured a spirited competition in which local businessmen vied for the dubious distinction of being named Miss Slush Pit.

Not only was the first oil well in Northwest Louisiana drilled in this area, but the world's first marine well was drilled in nearby Caddo Lake. Until May 1911, when this original offshore well was completed, underwater drilling remained in the realm of theory.

Water sports enthusiasts will appreciate Caddo Lake for other reasons. The large, cypress-studded lake, which can be reached via Route 1, offers opportunities for boating, skiing, fishing, hunting, and camping. Consulting your map you'll see that the lake also spills over into Texas.

Continue south to Mooringsport and pick up Route 169. At the junction of Route 169 north and Blanchard-Furrh Road, you'll see the ◆ **Stumpwater Inn Restaurant**. This family restaurant, decorated in a country theme with shelves of old farm tools and mounted heads of deer, features good country cooking with a Cajun flavor. Even if it's not mealtime, stop anyway and order coffee and a piece of pie—either French kiss if you're a chocolate lover or the restaurant's popular lemon icebox. In polls conducted by a Shreveport newspaper, the Stumpwater came out on top for its homemade desserts and placed in all other categories. Not only that, the inn's waitresses won the award for "Best in Service." *Portfolio* (another Shreveport publication) ranked "our catfish the best in North Louisiana," says Lloyd Saunders, who with his wife Judy owns the eatery.

You may want to try the lobster thermidor, one of the Stumpwater's own specialties, or Neptune casserole, a tasty combination of crab and shrimp with lobster thermidor sauce over baked fettuccine. Catfish and steaks are perennial favorites. The Stumpwater features an all-you-can-eat seafood buffet on Tuesday and Friday from 5:00 P.M. to closing. Hours are 10:00 A.M. to 9:00 P.M. Sunday through Thursday, and 10:00 A.M. until 10:00 P.M. Friday and Saturday. Prices are economical to moderate. The Stumpwater closes on Mondays. Call (318) 929–3725.

Continue to 8012 Blanchard-Furrh Road, where you'll find the ◈ **Walter B. Jacobs Memorial Nature Park**—2.9 miles east of Longwood (Route 169) and 2.8 miles west of Blanchard (Route 173). Dedicated to nature's preservation, the park invites those who want to use it for walking, hiking, photography, painting, writing, bird-watching, or simply the pure enjoyment of being outdoors.

At the interpretive building you'll see an exhibit on predators and prey, coiled live snakes in glass cages, and a colony of bees in action. Other displays feature mounted specimens of native wildlife such as a Louisiana black bear, coyotes, and river otters. One of the building's classrooms contains "feel" boxes, helpful for using a hands-on approach with students. Youngsters can reach inside a box, guess what object they're touching, and then describe it for their classmates. This leads to follow-up discussions on different aspects of nature. (I was relieved that my box contained an antler instead of something squirmy.)

Trail and terrain maps are given to visitors who want to hike through the 160-acre park of hickory, pine, and oak trees. Markers identify natural features and animal habitats along the trails. Local woods are populated by deer, snakes, lizards, turtles, rabbits, squirrels, opossums, raccoons, armadillos, and other animals.

The park provides a picnic area for people who want to pack a lunch and spend the day. Also, a full-time naturalist is available

4

to arrange guided tours, present programs, teach sessions, and, in general, share his expertise.

You can visit from 8:00 A.M. to 5:00 P.M. Wednesday through Saturday and from 1:00 to 5:00 P.M. on Sunday. The park is closed New Year's Day, Easter, Thanksgiving, and Christmas Day. Admission is free. Call the park naturalist at (318) 929–2806 for more information.

After a hiking session through the park, you'll probably be ready for another meal. If so, head into Shreveport where the staff of ◆ **Freeman and Harris Cafe** at 317 Western Avenue will make you glad you came. Look for a building with a yellow brick front and orange and yellow trim. Noted for its Southern-style soul food, the restaurant has been doing a brisk business at this location since 1936. Stevie Wonder made it a point to seek out Freeman and Harris Cafe when he visited Shreveport.

Be sure to ask about the luncheon specials offered Monday through Friday from 11:00 A.M. to 2:30 P.M. Tasty options may include fried chicken, chops, chicken and dumplings, chicken-fried steak, turnip greens, black-eyed peas, and other Southern favorites.

Sample the crab, trout, or stuffed shrimp (for which the restaurant is famous). Another good choice is the cafe's special broiled shrimp in creamy sauce with sautéed onions and bell peppers. Or you might try another house specialty, red beans and rice with ham hock. The restaurant, which is open from 8:00 A.M. to 2 A.M. Sunday through Thursday and from 8:00 A.M. to 3:00 A.M. on Friday and Saturday, also makes deliveries. Call (318) 425–7786 for more information.

After a fine meal some mild exercise is always in order. A pleasant way to get it is to visit the ◆ **American Rose Center** at 8877 Jefferson-Paige Road. Located just off Interstate 20, the American Rose Center is 5 miles east of the Texas state line and about 10 miles west of downtown Shreveport. Take exit 5 and follow the signs.

Now America's national flower (Congress made it official in 1986), the rose reigns supreme here at America's largest rose garden. The American Rose Society, which celebrated its one hundredth birthday in 1992, also makes its headquarters at the center. You can stroll along pathways edged by split-rail fences to see nine theme gardens of roses at this facility that spreads over

118 acres. You don't have to be a rose expert to appreciate the beauty of this place. A label next to each planting provides such pertinent information as the rose's name, type, and heritage. Like the flowers themselves, the names are intriguing: White Masterpiece, New Year, Show Biz, French Lace, Angel Face, Touch of Class, Double Delight, and Sweet Surrender are among the rose varieties you can see here. While sampling this buffet of blossoms, be careful when you sniff—bees like the roses, too.

The Windsounds Carillon Tower rises impressively from plantings of award-winning roses in reds, pinks, yellows, mauves, and a medley of other colors. You'll also find a picturesque log cabin chapel, a gift shop, sundials, gazebos, inviting benches, and picnicking facilities.

Christmas in Roseland makes the place more magical than ever with such entertainment as choral groups, soloists, dancers, and storytellers. Displays include illuminated wire sculptures depicting the Nativity scene, Eiffel Tower, Statue of Liberty, a spotlighted group of sixty large wooden Christmas card panels designed and painted by area students, a model train exhibit, and other festive displays.

You can visit the Rose Center from mid-April through October between 9:00 A.M. and 6:00 P.M. daily. Holiday hours, from Thanksgiving through New Year's Eve (except for Christmas Day), change to 5:30 till 10:00 P.M. Admission is modest. Call (318) 938–5402.

The ◆ **Grass Roots Country Cottage** at 1259 Ellerbe Road, some 13 miles south of downtown Shreveport, will transport you to a world of rustic charm. Nita and Larry Rogers converted a house on their property into a lovely bed and breakfast cottage that offers one bedroom with private bath. French doors lead to a deck where you can sit with your morning coffee and enjoy the country landscape of green pastures bordered by split-rail fences. The cottage (with a decor that Nita describes as "country") looks as if it should be featured in a home-decorating magazine. "Like Barbara Mandrell," Nita says, "I was country before country was cool." Handmade quilts, plump cushions, house plants, and wicker rockers make the place so inviting that most guests don't want to leave. (One high-tech consultant had booked the cottage for two nights, but after reveling in the serenity, he wanted to double that time. Nita only persuaded him to depart because she had more company coming!)

Overnight guests are welcomed with a cheese tray and lemonade. Breakfast is served in the cottage's dining room, which also is open to the public for lunch on Friday and Saturday. Lunch offers a choice of two entrées, one of which will feature crepes (a house specialty) filled with turkey, chicken, ham, or beef; homemade soup; a vegetable; congealed (gelatin) salad; cornbread muffins *and* hot yeast rolls; plus dessert and beverage. Prices are moderate. Call (318) 797–1005 for reservations or additional information.

If you travel north from Grass Roots for twenty minutes, you'll arrive in the heart of Shreveport, now big and bustling. The city truly qualified as an off-the-beaten-path kind of place before Captain Henry Miller Shreve appeared on the scene in 1833 to unclog the Red River. Using snag boats, Shreve and his crews divested the river of a log jam known as the "Great Raft," which extended some 180 miles—a project that took five years and cost $300,000. Later the town that sprang up on the banks of the Red River was named in honor of Captain Shreve.

The Louisiana legislature officially recognized Shreveport as a town in 1839. During the Civil War Shreveport served as the state's capital for a short time. The last place in Louisiana to concede defeat, its official Confederate flag was not lowered until Federal troops arrived to occupy the city.

Start your visit to Shreveport with a drive through the historical Highland-Fairfield area, a setting for many of the city's elegant mansions. Fairfield Avenue, one of Shreveport's most attractive streets, features grand houses in a diversity of architectural styles. One of these lovely homes, ◆ **Fairfield Place** in the city's Highland Historic District, can be your base while here. When Janie Lipscomb first saw this classic Victorian house located at 2221 Fairfield Avenue, she fell in love with it and immediately signed a sales contract on the hood of her car.

With two crews of carpenters and craftsmen, she worked day and night seven days a week for the next five months to restore the home and convert it into an elegant guest house. The bed and breakfast facility was opened in 1983. Dating from the 1870s, the home still contains many of its original brass light fixtures and much of its copper hardware.

A former dental hygienist, Janie's effervescence and energy serve her well in her current career as innkeeper. "I've tried to give each room everything I ever wanted in a hotel room," she says, "and eliminate everything I hate about hotel rooms." Her special touches include European feather beds (both comfortable and nonallergenic) and New Zealand wool rugs. Fairfield Place's nine spacious guest rooms, including a suite with private parlor, are individually decorated with European and American antiques and are supplied with plenty of good reading material, and even terry bathrobes. All bedrooms have private baths (some with antique footed tubs). Janie succeeds in her quest of inviting you "to relax and enjoy the quiet, casually elegant atmosphere."

King-size beds, color television sets, digital alarm clocks, and telephones are all standard equipment in this hostelry. Janie has even remembered all the little extras—French soaps, eye makeup remover, and fresh flowers from her garden. (Janie's an avid gardener, and you will admire her well-kept grounds and lovely bedding plants.)

Janie serves weekday breakfasts at 7:15 A.M. (to accommodate business travelers) and at 8:00 A.M. on weekends. When you smell the rich Cajun coffee, you can step outside your door to the large hall to serve yourself from the antique English armoire in the downstairs hall or from the English sideboard buffet upstairs. Colorful cloth napkins, pretty china, and sterling silver flatware all enhance the quiche, home-baked croissants filled with a tasty ham and cheese mixture, or one of Janie's other delectable recipes, which she gladly shares with guests. Bran or marmalade muffins, juice, strawberry butter, and assorted jellies complete the meal. You can either take your tray to a table in your room or sit on the front porch or balcony to enjoy breakfast. House policies prohibit smoking.

Rates are moderate and credit cards are accepted. Call (318) 222–0048 for reservations or additional information.

A trek into traffic will reward you with some special places that would be a shame to miss. You'll get a real feel for the city's history at the ◆ **Spring Street Museum,** located at 525 Spring Street. Built as a bank in 1866 and recently restored, this fine structure with its cast-iron balcony is one of the town's oldest existing buildings. An eight-minute video presentation acquaints you with the city's early history. Rotating exhibits allow the museum to showcase its historical collections of furniture, clothing, jewelry, firearms, books, and newspapers. When I visited, an extensive exhibit of elegant vintage clothing was on display, and a newspaper dated September 10, 1935, screamed the news that Senator Huey Long (nicknamed the "Kingfish") had died—he had been shot at the state capitol two days before.

Don't miss seeing the upstairs with its permanent collection of Victorian furnishings. Beautiful period pieces include American Chippendale chairs that date from 1760 to 1775, paintings from the 1800s, various pieces of carved rosewood furniture, an 1878 cherry and walnut organ that has been restored to playing condition, a child's harp, a melodeon, and a Persian carpet. You'll also see a velvet-covered chair that belonged to Shreveport's famous madam (who received a three-month bank loan for her business and repaid it within two weeks).

While in the area you can stop for a meal at ✤ **The Blind Tiger** on the corner of Spring and Texas streets in historical Shreve Square. Harking back to the time of Prohibition and speakeasies when saloons operated behind façades or "blinds" such as museums with wild animal displays to mask back rooms where alcoholic beverages were sold, the restaurant's name serves as a reminder of the town's past.

Now owned by Joey Kent, the building was erected in 1848, burned in 1854, and rebuilt later to house several businesses including the Buckelew Hardware Company. The interior echoes the nostalgic theme with stained glass, dark wood paneling, brass rails, and Tiffany chandeliers. Displayed in the Tiger's Den, you'll see a wall of vintage photos depicting Shreveport's early days.

"Our menu offers plenty of variety, although the emphasis is on seafood," says Rick Sloan, who with Glenn Brannan owns The Blind Tiger. Consider an appetizer of tiger wings or pigskins for starters, then try the house spinach salad topped with grilled beef or chicken kebabs. Seafood lovers may want to order the snapper creole. The restaurant also serves great steaks and hamburgers. In a local reader survey, The Blind Tiger's chicken salad ranked among the best in the Shreveport-Bossier area, and the cheesecake won first place. Prices are moderate. Hours are from 11:00 A.M. to 10:00 P.M. Monday through Thursday and 11:00 P.M. on Friday, 5:00 to 11:00 P.M. on Saturday, and noon to 9:00 P.M. on Sunday. Call (318) 226–8747.

Located at 619 Louisiana Avenue, the ✤ **Strand Theatre** is a must-see, although parking can present a problem. Be sure to notice the dome and the exterior's decorative details as you approach. Now restored to its previous grandeur, the neo–baroque theater originally opened in 1925 with the operetta *The Chocolate Soldier*. Listed on the National Register of Historic Places, the 1,640-seat theater boasts an organ of 939 pipes, ornate box seats, a goldfish pond, and gilt-edged mirrors. The interior features a color scheme of rich burgundy with gold accents. Don't forget to look up at the magnificent ceiling and dazzling chandeliers.

Since it reopened in 1984, this downtown landmark again attracts crowds for performances that range from ballet and musical extravaganzas on ice to touring Broadway hits. The Strand is open for performances or by appointment. Call (318) 226–1481.

Continue to the ◆**Meadows Museum of Art,** located at 2911 Centenary Boulevard on the Centenary College campus. The museum features a fascinating one-man collection of Indochinese art. Don't miss the museum's award-winning film, *Indochina Revisited: A Portrait of Jean Despujols*. This twenty-eight-minute documentary will provide some glimpses into the life and work of an extraordinary artist.

From December 1936 to August 1938, French artist Jean Despujols made his way through French Indochina's interior, capturing its people and landscapes with pastel, oil, charcoal, and watercolor. This rare collection of 360 works is personalized by excerpts from a diary he kept while traveling through the remote areas of Vietnam, Laos, and Cambodia. Despujols moved to Shreveport in 1941 and became an American citizen in 1945. His collection (hidden at his parents' home in France) survived World War II only to disappear in transit later when the artist requested that it be shipped to him in America. Lost for seven months during the trip from France, the valuable collection surfaced in Guadeloupe, where it had mistakenly been unloaded. The treasure finally arrived in Shreveport in December 1948.

The Smithsonian Institution exhibited Despujols's works in 1950, and *National Geographic* borrowed twenty-one of his paintings to illustrate a 1951 article on Indochina. Despujols died in 1965, and his works were kept in a Shreveport bank vault. In 1969 Centenary alumnus Algur H. Meadows purchased the collection, presented it to the college, and also provided funds for a museum to house the rare body of work.

The Meadows Museum also displays major traveling exhibits

throughout the year. The museum is open to the public from 1:00 to 5:00 P.M. Tuesday through Friday and from 1:00 to 4:00 P.M. Saturday and Sunday. Admission is free. For more information, call (318) 869–5169.

After a visit to the museum, take Route 1 to the campus of Louisiana State University in Shreveport. At 8515 Youree Drive (near the northeast corner of the campus), you'll find the ◆ **Pioneer Heritage Center**. The complex is composed of several authentic plantation structures that give you a picture— outside the pages of a history book—of how the area's early settlers lived.

The **Webb and Webb Commissary** serves as a visitors' center where you'll get an overview of the operation and an interesting history lesson about the pioneers who settled the northwest corner of Louisiana. The building itself is typical of a company store in an agricultural community where purchases could be made on credit before a crop was harvested and paid off later when the crop was sold.

You'll come away with a new appreciation for modern dentistry after seeing the dental drill displayed in the doctor's office

Webb and Webb Commissary

11

at the Pioneer Heritage Center. There's also a collection of medical and surgical instruments from the "olden days." One room contains displays of various herbal home remedies.

Docents dressed in period clothing demonstrate pioneer skills, which range from churning butter to making bricks as they interpret life from the 1830s period and provide eye-opening experiences for youngsters and adults. Students can try making a clay and straw "cat" for a chimney or run up a few stitches in a quilt stretched on a frame.

You'll see the restored 1856 "Big House," a frame antebellum cottage from Caspiana Plantation, and an outside kitchen. A nearby structure, the Thrasher log house, illustrates the dogtrot style. The dogtrot (an open passage supposedly favored by the family dogs) provided a cool covered area for performing household chores during hot weather. The complex also features an equipped blacksmith's shop.

Jointly sponsored by the university and the Junior League of Shreveport, the Pioneer Heritage Center closes for major holidays and from mid-December through February. Visiting hours are Sundays from 1:30 to 4:30 P.M. or weekdays by appointment (groups only). Admission is modest, and children get in for free. Call (318) 797–5332 for more information.

At ◆ **Dudley and Gerald's South Louisiana Kitchen,** located at 2421 East Seventieth Street, you can sample special Cajun dishes in a North Louisiana locale. Owner Dudley Vallot offers such delights as court bouillon (koo boo-YON), crawfish stew, shrimp, oyster or catfish po-boys (submarine sandwiches for "poor boys"), stuffed crab, and jambalaya. You also can opt for steaks—a rib eye or a filet mignon that comes with french fries and coleslaw.

If it's lunchtime and you're in a hurry, order from the items with stars—they require less time to prepare. Try Gerald's shrimp fettuccine or the Louisiana fried oysters with jambalaya.

The restaurant, open Monday through Sunday, operates from 11:30 A.M. until 10:00 P.M. You can call (318) 797–3010 for more information.

Before continuing east, you may want to sweep south a short distance for a look at a charming little town called Keatchie (KEY-chi—the second syllable sounds like the *chi* in "child").

DeSoto Parish

To reach ◆**Keatchie,** about 25 miles southwest of Shreveport, take U.S. Highway 171 south (the Mansfield Road), then turn west on State Route 5. Incorporated in 1858 as Keachi, the town takes its name from a Native American tribe of Caddo ancestry. You may see a sign that says WELCOME TO HISTORIC KEATCHI because Travis Whitfield and other members of the local heritage foundation want to see the original spelling restored.

Predominantly Greek Revival, which Travis describes as "kind of a Parthenon temple style," much of the town's architecture dates to the 1840s and 1850s and is on the National Register of Historic Places. On a driving tour, you'll see three Greek Revival–style churches, the large Keatchie Plantation Store, the Masonic Hall, and a Confederate cemetery. On Highway 172 west of downtown stands the 1852 Keatchie Baptist Church, originally the chapel for a women's college (no longer in existence). Also, on what was once the campus, you'll see a building that was recently moved here to serve as a future cultural center.

Afterward, you can head southeast to historic Natchitoches (described in the section on Central Louisiana, p. 44) via Interstate 49 or return to Shreveport for an eastward thrust.

Bossier Parish

Traveling east, Bossier City begins where Shreveport ends. Bossier boasts a well-beaten path, Louisiana Downs, one of the country's top racetracks for thoroughbreds.

The ◆**Touchstone Wildlife and Art Museum** is located 2.2 miles east of the Louisiana Downs Race Track on U.S. Highway 80 near Bossier City. Founded by professional taxidermists Lura and Sam Touchstone, this natural history museum features hand-painted dioramas as backdrops for mounted mammals, birds, and reptiles from all over the world. The collection contains more than 1,000 specimens of wildlife displayed in habitats simulating their natural environments. Sam practices "taxidermy in action," and all his animals are engaged in lifelike pursuits. Be sure to notice the giraffe, the family of red fox, and the 310-pound gorilla (the latter died at age twenty-seven in a zoo).

One coastline setting shows an exhibit of brown pelicans, which may be the only ones you see in the Pelican State. (Once plentiful, Louisiana's state bird fell victim to pesticides, and the unfortunate result was a drastic decrease in the pelican population.)

Also on display are collections of insects, Native American artifacts, war relics, and antique tools. The museum is open Tuesday through Saturday from 9:00 A.M. until 5:00 P.M. and on Sunday from 1:00 to 5:00 P.M. Parking is free, and admission is modest. Call (318) 949-2323.

WEBSTER PARISH

Continue east from Bossier City, either by way of Interstate 20 or U.S. Highways 79–80, and you'll arrive in Minden. Take time to drive along Minden's brick streets to see the downtown area with antique shops and several homes on the National Register of Historic Places.

Located 7 miles northeast of Minden (and some 30 miles east of Shreveport), you'll find the ◆ **Germantown Colony Museum** on Route 114. Several German families established a village here in 1835, and their furniture, documents, letters, tools, and other artifacts are exhibited both in replica buildings and in original cabins made of hand-hewn logs.

On display is a copy of an 1826 document signed by an archduke ordering Count von Leon (who became the group's leader) to leave Germany. In Pennsylvania the count and his wife met other German families who shared similar religious beliefs. They joined forces and began a journey south to the Minden area, the site they selected to establish a community. During the trip the count died of yellow fever at Grand Encore, Louisiana. Undaunted, the countess carried on and saw the group's goal of establishing a self-sufficient religious colony fulfilled. Germantown functioned as a communal system for more than three and a half decades. The countess earned money by giving music lessons. (Her pupils came from Minden.) Other colonists performed work according to their talents and interests. The group grew grape and mulberry trees for making jellies and wine.

You'll see the cabin where the countess lived and the kitchen-dining hall where the colonists gathered for meals, as well as reproductions of a smokehouse (on the site of the original), a doctor's cottage, and a blacksmith shop with authentic equipment. All the buildings contain items that the Germantown settlers used, and a map shows where other structures, such as barns and workhouses, once stood.

On the walls of the countess's cabin, you can see remnants of the original wallpaper that she ordered from New Orleans. Among the interesting items on display are the countess's piano, Count von Leon's coronet, the colony's book of laws, German Bibles, ledgers, and slave passes.

The museum is open Wednesday through Saturday from 9:00 A.M. until 5:00 P.M. Sunday hours are from 1:00 to 6:00 P.M. Admission is modest. For additional information you can call (318) 377–1875.

Traveling east from Webster Parish takes you to a part of Louisiana known as Piney Hills Country, a large region that encompasses the parishes of Bienville, Claiborne, Jackson, Lincoln, Union, and Winn. From Minden take U.S. Highway 80 east until it intersects Route 154.

BIENVILLE PARISH

Travel south on Route 154 toward Mount Lebanon. This community holds an annual Stagecoach Trail Tour of its antebellum homes the first Sunday in May. Located on a downtown corner, the Stagecoach Museum is open Friday through Sunday from 2:00 to 5:00 P.M.

From Mount Lebanon continue south for 5 miles. Here under Ambrose Mountain's shady pines stands a simple marker denoting the ◆**Bonnie and Clyde Ambush Site.** The notorious couple had vowed never to be taken alive. At this spot a surprise attack by Texas Rangers brought the fugitives' spree of bank robberies to a screeching halt. The stone marker, erected by the Bienville Parish Police Jury, reads AT THIS SITE MAY 23, 1934, CLYDE BARROW AND BONNIE PARKER WERE KILLED BY LAW ENFORCEMENT OFFICIALS.

One local legend has it that during an attempted robbery of a Ruston bank, the couple took an undertaker as hostage. Clyde's bargain: the man's life for his future services. He was released in Arkansas when Clyde extracted a promise from the mortician to

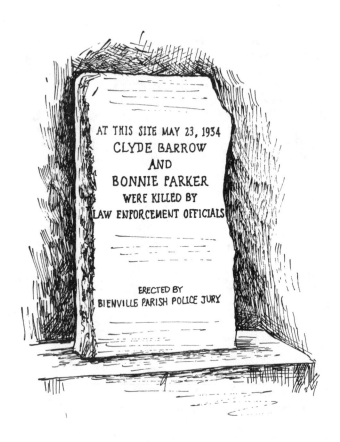

AT THIS SITE MAY 23, 1934
CLYDE BARROW
AND
BONNIE PARKER
WERE KILLED BY
LAW ENFORCEMENT OFFICIALS

ERECTED BY
BIENVILLE PARISH POLICE JURY

Bonnie and Clyde Ambush Site

make him "look good" after the inevitable occurred. Later, upon learning the couple had been killed, the undertaker traveled to the Arcadia funeral home (where the bodies had been taken), determined to keep his end of the bargain. Although he found the two corpses beyond salvaging, he was allowed to restore one of Clyde's hands.

After your visit return to Mt. Lebanon and continue north where you will intersect U.S. Highway 80. Travel east on this road until you reach Arcadia. This small town, along with nearby

Homer, Athens, and Sparta, all took their names from ancient Greek towns.

Bienville Parish pays tribute to its marsupial population each June by staging a **Possum Festival** in Arcadia. Fun-filled activities scheduled during this popular event include a possum auction, an outdoor banquet, horseshoe-pitching contests, mud volleyball, and a golf tournament.

In Arcadia the populace remains divided regarding a museum featuring Bonnie and Clyde memorabilia. Some, remembering the terror inspired by this gun-slinging couple, oppose the idea of displays that might seem to romanticize their heinous crimes. The opposite faction insists that the criminal careers of Bonnie and Clyde are part of local history; people want to know about this, so why not market it? The Parish Historical Society is currently renovating the downtown depot circa 1884. This structure, the ◆**Bienville Depot Museum,** will house a permanent exhibit of memorabilia related to Bonnie and Clyde, including a collection of unpublished photos owned by area residents.

If you pass through Arcadia before the museum opens, you can stop by the **Bienville Parish Courthouse** (next door to the depot) where some artifacts related to Bonnie and Clyde are now kept. As you can imagine, the ambush photos (which fall in the sanguinary category) are not displayed for general public viewing; however, they are shown on request.

Homer, located 23 miles north of Arcadia, can be reached by taking Route 9 north, which runs into U.S. Highway 79 just outside the town.

CLAIBORNE PARISH

Proceed to Homer's town square. On the square's south side, you'll see the ◆**Ford Museum,** located at 519 South Main Street. It might be said that this museum owes its existence to a German infantry officer's helmet, which inspired the museum's collection. When Herbert S. Ford's sons retrieved the helmet from the town dump, he embarked on a personal campaign to preserve for posterity other items of historical significance.

In 1918 Ford started a collection, and as he accumulated additional artifacts, storage became a problem. At various times the collection occupied a room at the local high school, a railroad car, and the town hall. This remarkable assemblage now has a permanent home in the handsome Hotel Claiborne, a building that dates from 1890.

The museum's displays focus on local history. Downstairs you will see interpretative exhibits for each of the area's major development stages, starting with a dugout canoe from the Indian period. Illustrating the parish's pioneer period is an authentic log cabin moved from nearby Haynesville. The structure had to be dismantled and then reassembled inside the museum. Other interesting exhibits include a moonshiner's still for making corn whiskey, a blacksmith's forge, a corn sheller, and a cotton scale.

The museum also features a collection of thirty plantation bells, which came from schools and farms throughout the parish. This exhibit will certainly get your attention if your visit happens to coincide with that of touring youngsters, who love to hear the bells do what bells are supposed to do.

Don't miss the upstairs area, where individual rooms carry out various themes. You'll see a series of historical settings featuring a doctor's office and pharmacy, a chapel room, school, general store, military room, and the like. Also on display are antique firearms (including Confederate weapons) and a doctor's buggy that was used in an old John Wayne movie, *The Horse Soldiers*, filmed in nearby Natchitoches.

Even though the Ford Museum could be considered off the beaten path, about two thousand persons find their way to this fascinating facility each year. Community volunteers serve as guides and play a major role in the museum's operation. Weekday hours are from 8:00 A.M. to 1:00 P.M. and from 2:00 to 4:00 P.M. On Sundays you can visit between 2:00 and 5:00 P.M. Admission is modest. Call (318) 927–3271 for more information.

From the Ford Museum you can walk across the street to the ◆ **Claiborne Parish Courthouse,** in the middle of Homer's town square. A classic example of Greek Revival architecture, the structure was completed in 1861 and is still in use. The courthouse served as the departure point for area soldiers mustering for the Confederate cause and remains one of only four pre–Civil War courthouses in Louisiana. Some artifacts from the courthouse are displayed at the Ford Museum.

Near Summerfield some 16 miles northeast of Homer via Route 9, you'll find the **Aïberry Wasson Homeplace.** If time permits you might want to visit this 1850 home, which is the only two-story double-dogtrot log house in the state. Now restored, the house contains family antiques and exhibits related to the area's history. Be sure to call ahead for an appointment because the house is not open on a regular basis. The number is (318) 927–2754. Admission is modest.

From Homer, take Route 146 southeast to Vienna and pick up U.S. 167 south, which leads to Ruston.

LINCOLN PARISH

You are now in peach country. From mid-March through early April, this region becomes a landscape of blooming peach trees. Joe Mitcham's Peach Orchard, located just outside Ruston on routes 181 and 182, offers fresh peaches for sale during June.

Ruston hosts the annual **Louisiana Peach Festival,** which has been chosen one of the Southeast Tourism Society's top twenty events for June. Besides eating lots of peach ice cream, festival-goers can enjoy a parade, treasure hunt, auction, cooking contests, craft exhibits, and musical entertainment.

Founded in 1884 as Russ Town, the city was named for Robert E. Russ, who gave the Vicksburg, Shreveport, and Pacific Railroad some acreage to build a railroad and townsite on his property. An early center of culture, Ruston was the site of the Louisiana Chautauqua, a summer program providing opportunities for citizens to immerse themselves in music, drama, art, and the like. The town is now home to two universities, Grambling and Louisiana Tech.

The ◆**Lincoln Parish Museum,** located at 609 North Vienna Street, serves as a good starting point to begin your exploration of this inviting city. Housed in the lovely Kidd-Davis home built in 1886, the regional museum features a collection of period furniture, paintings, and other items of historical interest. In the entry hall be sure to notice the hand-painted wall murals that illustrate the Chautauqua and scenes from local history.

You'll see a dollhouse, exquisitely furnished with tiny period pieces, on display downstairs and another on the second floor. The museum's upstairs exhibits are changed seasonally to feature various collections such as vintage wedding dresses or original textiles designed during the 1930s as part of the government's Works Progress Administration program. Other displays include household items ranging from cornshuck brooms and kitchen utensils to antique radios and tools.

The Ruston-Lincoln Chamber of Commerce and the Lincoln Parish Visitors Bureau also are located here. Pick up a self-guided tour brochure on Ruston's Historic District and take a walking or driving tour of the neighborhood's tree-lined streets. Ruston's north-south streets were named for nearby towns, and the east-west avenues take their names from Southern states. Local attractions are clustered and make for easy sightseeing.

The museum is open Monday through Friday from 8:30 A.M. to noon and from 1:00 to 5:00 P.M., and on Saturday and Sunday by appointment. Call (318) 251–0018 or (318) 255–2031 for more information.

If you're in Ruston on a Saturday night, it would be unthinkable to miss the Dixie Jamboree. Jimmy Howard heads up this show and guarantees a knee-slapping, toe-tapping good time for all. The weekly musical review is staged at 206 North Vienna Street in the ◆ **Dixie Theater.** Originally an old movie house, the theater was built around 1920 and has been restored. Be sure to notice the auditorium's beautiful chandelier.

The weekly show features singer-hostess Myrtle Branch, the Dixie Jamboree Band, and guest performers (who audition the previous Thursday). Their lively music sends many couples to the dance floor just below the stage. Selections range from traditional country and gospel to blues and old standards. Live entertainment also may include comedians and dancers. The show, which starts at 7:00 P.M., is held every Saturday night year-round. Admission is modest. Call (318) 255–6081.

Health permitting, former Louisiana governor and professional gospel singer Jimmie Davis puts in an occasional appearance at the Dixie Jamboree, and it's always a sellout. Davis also pays an annual visit to a Homecoming held at the **Jimmie Davis Tabernacle,** south of Ruston in Jackson Parish. The revival-style Homecoming, which is held the first Sunday in October, attracts lots of folks. Everyone is invited to bring a covered dish and enjoy an old-fashioned dinner on the grounds. (At many places in the South, lunch is called "dinner," and dinner is called "supper.")

One of Davis's original songs, "You Are My Sunshine," became a hit in 1939 and was later recorded in thirty-four languages. Professional gospel groups from across the country join the singing governor for this function held on the site of Davis's parents' home close to the Peckerwood Hill Store. The Tabernacle, built in 1965 by a group of Davis's friends, is located near the junction of highways 542 and 811 midway between Quitman and Jonesboro.

In Ruston be sure to stop by the ◆ **Piney Hills Gallery,** located on the ground floor of the historic Harris Hotel building (reputed to be haunted) at 206 Park Avenue. Original works, ranging from traditional and contemporary crafts to fine arts by North Central Louisiana artists, are displayed in this consignment sales gallery.

You'll see paintings, pottery, furniture, quilts, crocheted items, cornshuck hats, walking sticks, hunting horns, dolls, stuffed toys, puppets, stained glass, jewelry, lamps, sculpture, calligraphy, and photography. Also on display are baskets of split white oak, textile arts, wood carvings, and handmade musical instruments. Homemade jellies and relishes are for sale.

Unique pieces from the Follette Studio and Odell Pottery are among the gallery's distinctive offerings. Kent Follette, a nationally acclaimed potter, maintains a studio on Route 455, 4 miles north of Ruston, which is open from 10:00 A.M. through 5:00 P.M. Monday through Saturday. Call him at (318) 251–1310 for more information.

Bruce Odell's Pottery Studio, located at 1705 Kentucky Avenue West, is also open to the public. Visitors are welcome from 10:00 A.M. to 6:00 P.M. throughout the week. Representing the United States in 1992, Bruce and his wife Tami traveled to Italy for the International Pottery Olympics and returned with a gold medal. Bruce's unique clay creations, decorated by Tami, beat out all competition in the aesthetics division. He also placed in the top ten in the technical division. Odell's Louisiana Tech students often work at his studio, which contains a showroom as well as a display of rejected pottery in a nearby shed. To the untrained eye, many of these seconds contain no flaws, and they are sold at reduced rates. (I bought a beautiful vase, platter, and lamp base for less than $70.00.)

The Piney Hills Gallery staff provides a referral service for customers who want to see more of a particular artist's work. Articles at the gallery can range in price from $2.00 to $2,000.00. The gallery is open from 10:00 A.M. until 4:00 P.M. Tuesday through Saturday, and closes on holidays. Special appointments for other hours can be made by calling (318) 255–7234 during gallery hours.

After leaving the gallery take time to stop by ◆ **Erma's,** nearby at 109 North Trenton. Owner Kim Davis offers an array of sandwiches, soups, and salads such as a grilled chicken salad, a green salad served with baked brie on bread, and a dieter's selection. Other popular choices include the prime rib sandwich, quiche, and her shrimp puff. Whichever you choose, save room for dessert, such as flan with rich almond sauce or Erma's ever-popular praline cheesecake. Prices are economical. The restaurant is open Monday through Friday from 11:00 A.M. until 2:00 P.M. Call (318) 251–1879.

At some point during your Ruston visit, plan to stop by the ◆ **Log Cabin Smokehouse,** located a quarter of a mile north of Interstate 20 at 1906 Farmerville Highway. Housed in an 1886 dogtrot home of hand-hewn logs, the eatery serves barbecue sandwiches or hickory smoked beef, turkey breast, ham, pork ribs, chicken, and sausage. Texas toast, hickory smoked beans, and coleslaw or potato salad complete your meal. Prices are economical. From Monday through Thursday, serving hours run from 11:00 A.M. to 8:30 P.M. and to 9:00 P.M. on Friday and Saturday. Closed Sunday. Call (318) 255–8023.

Youngsters will enjoy seeing ◆ **Idea Place** in Woodard Hall on the campus of **Louisiana Tech University,** located on the town's west side. This children's museum features hands-on exhibits designed to encourage both you and the kids to investigate scientific and mathmatical concepts and have fun at the same time. For more information and hours, call the Ruston/Lincoln Convention and Visitors Bureau at (318) 255–2031.

The university offers a number of attractions, including a campus equine patrol. At Louisiana Tech Gallery in Wyly Tower, you can see displays of creations by local artists and craftspeople as well as traveling exhibits, Native American relics, pottery, and other area artifacts. Call (318) 257–3555 for more information.

Tech is also *the* place in Ruston to get ice cream—both cones and large containers—filled with such flavors as blueberry cheesecake and the old standbys vanilla, strawberry, and chocolate. During summer months you can enjoy peach ice cream, and at Christmastime, peppermint and rum raisin flavors are available. Thanks to the college's cows, you can also purchase other premium dairy products: fresh milk (including chocolate), cheeses, and butter along with rolls and bread—all at extremely reasonable prices. These products are sold daily at the Louisiana Tech Farm Salesroom, located behind Reese Hall (about 1.5 miles south of the main campus) just off U.S. Highway 80 west. You can line up with local students and professors Monday through Friday from 8:30 A.M. to 5:30 P.M. (With advance notice visitors can tour the nearby dairy plant, which processes these products.) Freshly cut roses at $2.00 a dozen are also available year-round at the Tech Farm Salesroom, but you need to arrive early because the flowers sell out fast.

Here on the Tech Farm campus close to the salesroom, you'll see the Horticultural Conservatory with more than 500 species of plants from all over the world. At Christmastime, the facility features a spectacular poinsettia show. Except for holidays, the conservatory is open by appointment only. Admission is free. Call (318) 257–2918 or (318) 257–3275.

Nearby you'll also see the Louisiana Tech Stallion Station (sometimes referred to as the Equine Center) where thoroughbreds and quarter horses are boarded, bred, and trained. You can tour the paddocks, barns, and stables, and if you arrive before 10:00 A.M., you can watch the horses being exercised. The center is open daily except during holidays, and there's no admission fee. Call (318) 257–4427.

Before leaving Ruston, you may want to indulge in some soul food at ◆ **Bee's Cafe,** located at 805 Larson Street. Bee's hotwater cornbread is scrumptious any time of the day—even at breakfast. Speaking of breakfast, this is a good place to fortify yourself for the rigors of the road. You can enjoy a pork chop (or bacon or sausage if you're a traditionalist) along with grits, eggs, and toast. A plate lunch might consist of smothered steak and vegetables (perhaps sweet potatoes or black-eyed peas), rice, and peach cobbler. All selections are written on a blackboard. Prices are economical. Hours are 5:30 A.M. to 6:30 P.M. Monday through Friday. Call (318) 255–5610.

NORTHEAST LOUISIANA

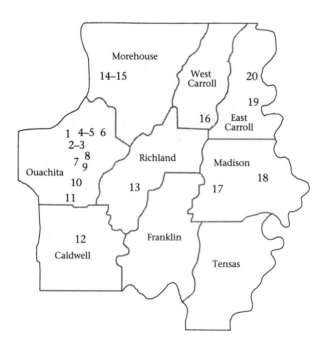

1. Kiroli Park
2. Ouachita River Art Guild Gallery
3. Antique Alley
4. Warehouse No. 1 Restaurant
5. Emy-Lou Biedenharn Foundation
6. Rebecca's Doll Museum
7. Masur Museum of Art
8. Layton Castle
9. Louisiana Purchase Gardens and Zoo
10. AGM Miniature Rose Farm
11. Boscobel Cottage
12. Louisiana Art & Folk Center and Museum
13. Bend of the River
14. The Johnson House
15. Snyder Memorial Museum and Creative Art Center
16. Poverty Point
17. Tensas River National Wildlife Refuge
18. Tallulah
19. Transylvania General Store
20. Ole Dutch Bakery

Northeast Louisiana

Ouachita Parish

After leaving Ruston travel east on Interstate 20 to West Monroe. You won't find a more inviting place to take a driving break than ❖ **Kiroli Park.** Located on Kiroli (ka-ROLL-ee) Road, the park's entrance is framed by tiers of flower beds. Nature trails for hiking and paved paths for jogging provide a pleasant interlude. The 126-acre park also features picnic facilities, tennis courts, a lodge, playgrounds, an amphitheater, a conservatory, and rest rooms.

Formerly used as a Boy Scout camp, the park is now owned and operated by the City of West Monroe. There's a modest admission fee; call (318) 396–4016.

For a look at original works by area artists, you can visit the ❖ **Ouachita River Art Guild Gallery** in Suite 20 at West Monroe's Glenwood Mall. Located at 102 Thomas Road, the fine art sales gallery features watercolor, oil, and acrylic paintings, photography, stained glass items, pottery, sculpture, jewelry, furniture, and other art forms. The gallery is open from 10:00 A.M. to 6:00 P.M. Tuesday through Saturday. For more information, call (318) 322–2380.

Antique buffs will want to save time for exploring ❖ **Antique Alley** in West Monroe. Between Trenton Street's one-hundred and three-hundred blocks, you'll find a concentration of antique and gift shops with more than twenty dealers, along with several art galleries and eateries. These renovated shops are housed in downtown buildings dating from the 1880s. Inventories feature American and European antiques, Oriental vases and rugs, silver, crystal, linens, primitives, baskets, railroad and nautical artifacts, quilts, Coca-Cola memorabilia, jewelry, coins, original paintings, and other decorative objects. Most shops are open Tuesday through Saturday from 10:00 A.M. until 5:00 P.M.

Continue east until West Monroe merges with Monroe. For a fine dinner, try ❖ **Warehouse No. 1 Restaurant** at One Olive Street. The eatery, which occupies a restored warehouse on the Ouachita (WASH-a-taw) River, features Louisiana seafood, catfish, and steaks. Specialties also include blackened jumbo shrimp, red snapper, or rib eye. If you dine early, 5:00 to 6:00 P.M. Monday through Saturday, the restaurant knocks $5.00 off all adult entrées. Prices are moderate to expensive. Call (318) 322–1340.

In Monroe head north to 2006 Riverside Drive, the location of the ◈ **Emy-Lou Biedenharn Foundation,** which consists of the Biedenharn family mansion, the Bible Museum (housing a remarkable collection of rare Bibles, books, illuminated manuscripts, musical instruments, and antique furnishings), and ELsong Gardens with piped music, splashing fountains, and a profusion of blooming plants.

A world-renowned concert contralto who once performed in Europe, Emy-Lou Biedenharn was forced to return to America when World War II brought her successful operatic career to an abrupt halt. Upon arriving at her Monroe home in 1939, her father, Joseph A. Biedenharn (Coca-Cola's first bottler), presented her with an original John Wycliffe Bible. This gift inspired her to

Emy-Lou Biedenharn Foundation

27

start collecting rare Bibles. She later bought the next-door mansion to contain her vast collection and named it ELsong (for "Emy-Lou's Song").

From the time you walk through the seven-hundred-pound solid bronze door (with its unique handle from an English castle), you realize you've entered a treasure trove.The priceless collection of bibles features a 1730 Martin Luther Bible written in German, a Bible edited by Thomas Jefferson, a "She" Bible, and a Bible illustrated by Salvador Dali. Other fascinating items include mosaics, handmade zithers, flutes, and Roman weapons. You'll also admire the silver urns, silk tapestries, Waterford crystal chandeliers, pier mirrors, and Tiffany plates.

The theme gardens are gorgeous. You'll see the Garden of Four Seasons with its marble cherubs, an Oriental garden featuring a gazebo and potted bonsai specimens, the Plants of the Bible Garden adjacent to the museum, the Ballet Lawn (where a bride was being photographed when I visited), and other delightful settings.

Except on national holidays, the facility is open Tuesday through Friday from 10:00 A.M. until 4:00 P.M. and on Saturday and Sunday from 2:00 until 5:00 P.M. Tours last about forty-five minutes and begin on the hour from 10:00 A.M. until 3:00 P.M. Tuesday through Friday and from 2:00 until 4:00 P.M. on Saturday and Sunday. Admission is free. Call (318) 387–5281 for more information.

Take time to drive through Monroe's square-mile **Historic District,** which overlooks the Ouachita River. Founded by Don Juan Filhiol, the original settlement was known as Fort Miro. Later the town's name was changed to Monroe in honor of the first steamboat to pass that way. Be sure to notice the Ouachita Parish Courthouse. At 520 South Grand Street, near the site of old Fort Miro, stands the frontier-style **Isaiah Garrett House.** This red-brick structure, which dates from 1840, contains memorabilia pertaining to local history and is open by appointment; call (318) 322–6192.

Near the stadium of Northeast Louisiana University, you'll find ◆ **Rebecca's Doll Museum** at 4500 Bon Aire Drive, the residence of the J. T. Balfours. The dolls are housed in a metal office building beside the home, and there's no sign. Jo Balfour does most of the showings and bookings, but the dolls belong to her daughter, Rebecca Ham.

You'll see more than two thousand dolls, most dating to the mid–1800s. Displayed in dollhouses, cabinets, and cradles, the delightful collection features antique dolls from Germany, France, and other countries. Also on exhibit is a unique wooden carving of Christ's Last Supper, sculpted by California artist Fred Thompson.

Rebecca started collecting dolls when she was thirteen, and the assemblage was first shown in 1976. Mrs. Balfour, who gives guided tours, says the museum is open "by appointment or by chance." Admission is modest. This stop takes less than an hour unless you're a doll collector and want to talk shop. For an appointment, call (318) 343–3361.

Continue to ◆ **Masur Museum of Art,** a modified English Tudor–style building at 1400 South Grand Street. In addition to the museum's permanent collection of paintings, graphics, sculpture, photographs, and other artworks, ten traveling exhibits are featured throughout the year.

A remodeled carriage house serves as an on-premises workshop for art classes. Trained volunteers conduct tours through the museum, which is open Tuesday through Thursday from 9:00 A.M. until 5:00 P.M. and Friday through Sunday from 2:00 until 5:00 P.M. Admission is free. Call (318) 329–2237.

At 1133 South Grand Street, you'll find ◆ **Layton Castle** with its fascinating feudal-like façade. The structure's commanding tower, arcaded gallery, and other unique features were added around 1910 when an earlier house was enclosed with rose-colored bricks, which were made on the grounds. Originally called Mulberry Grove (because the owner's silk industry required mulberry trees), Layton Castle began life as an 1814 raised cottage for Judge Henry Bry, one of Monroe's prominent early citizens.

Owner Carol Layton Parsons maintains the family mansion where impressive collections of antique furniture, family portraits, Audubon lithographs and chromolithographs, and other items of historical interest are housed. Portions of the enormous home have also been converted into apartments. Tours are conducted by appointment for groups of ten or more. Call Layton Castle Tours at (318) 343–1239.

Close by are the ◆ **Louisiana Purchase Gardens and Zoo** on Bernstein Drive. Here you can enjoy a delightful outing as you stroll tree-lined paths, take a leisurely cruise on a canopied pontoon, or chug around the park's Lewis and Clark Railroad via miniature steam locomotive. The Louisiana Territory's historic events and points of interest serve as the park's theme and a backdrop for an animal population that ranges between 750 and 850. Especially noted for its primate collection, the zoo's large group of lemurs (whose forebears came from Madagascar) were all bred on the premises.

As you cruise through varied settings that simulate the animals' natural habitats, you'll see the zoo's resident ham, Solomon, the llama. As your boat drifts by Solomon's pad, he rushes to the bank and strikes a pose for any photographers who may be aboard. And just in case they didn't get good shots, he lopes ahead a short distance and gives them another chance.

Several of the zoo's animals were transported to nearby Winnfield when the movie *Blaze* was being filmed. In one scene, a spider monkey named Juanita wanted to commend Paul Newman (who portrayed former Louisiana governor Earl K. Long) for his fine performance. Immediately after the actor delivered some lines to his stripper-girlfriend Blaze Starr, the monkey reached out of her cage and emphatically patted Newman on the shoulder.

Don't miss the snow leopard (with an unusual white tip on her tail), who was born at the zoo the day following the animals' acting debut. By consensus, she was named Blaze.

Among lush gardens with live oaks and a host of flowering plants, the zoo offers picnic huts and barbecue pits. Except for Thanksgiving and Christmas Day, the facility is open 10:00 A.M. until 5:00 P.M. daily. Admission is modest; children two and under are admitted free. Call (318) 329-2400.

Heading south to Bosco on U.S. Highway 165, you'll pass the ◆**AGM Miniature Rose Farm** at McDonald Lane. From here Gene King ships his award-winning miniature roses all over the country.

One rose is named Speechless, and this word could well describe most visitors when they walk into the first of the long greenhouses and see the vivid display of roses in reds, pinks, lavenders, oranges, apricots, whites, and multicolored blends. Gene, who recommends miniature roses for borders, planter boxes, pots, and as cut flowers, maintains they are "easier to grow" than other kinds of roses. The flowers boast imaginative names such as Hoddy Toddy (the fighting cheer for the Ole

Miss Rebels), Merrimac, Jim Dandy, Heartlight, Peaches 'N Cream, Fancy Pants, and Rainbow's End. Except when the flowers are dormant from mid-December to February, they bloom year-round. The roses put on their most spectacular show about mid-April.

Before you visit, call first to be sure Gene is home; the number is (318) 323–1219. For more information write AGM Miniature Roses, Inc., P.O. Box 6056, Monroe, LA 71211.

For a tranquil evening off the beaten path, make reservations at ✦ **Boscobel Cottage,** located about 14 miles south of Monroe off U. S. Highway 165 at 185 Cordell Lane. Owners Kay and Cliff LaFrance will welcome you to their lovely circa 1820 home. Originally built in a modified Federal–West Indies style, the plantation cottage was enlarged in 1840 and began to assume its present Greek Revival appearance. Both periods are reflected in the home's restoration and antique furnishings. The home, which retains much of its original glass and hardware, served as a residence for Judge Henry Bry when his nearby "big house," Boscobel (which no longer stands), was being built.

Kay and Cliff have converted the chapel beside Boscobel Cottage into a charming guest house, and when you arrive, you'll be greeted by family canines Jazz, Barker, Foxanne Marie and Mayhaw; as well as many mini-kitties. A host of felines, all with incredibly short legs, live on Boscobel's grounds. "A geneticist has speculated that these cats might be descendants of the kangaroo cats, popular in America during the 1920s," says Kay, a former evening-news anchorwoman for a Monroe television station.

Cliff, a pharmacist, whose past diversions have ranged from scuba diving under oil rigs in the Gulf of Mexico to playing tennis, now considers hosting his avocation. He will talk politics with you and relate some entertaining anecdotes. Speaking of politics, the family's cockatoo named Paco may tell you for whom to vote after he says "hello."

You'll enjoy strolling Boscobel's grounds and climbing the levee for a view of the Ouachita River. The levee is so inviting that sometimes when daughter Adrienne invites her friends to Boscobel (which means "beautiful woods"), they wrap up in quilts, mummy-fashion, and roll over and over down the slanting bank. On the grounds of Boscobel grow stately pecan trees, one of which has been designated the state's champion pecan tree.

Rates are moderate and include refreshments on arrival and a full breakfast with perhaps a pre-breakfast cup of coffee delivered to your door by Berta. You also can opt for a potluck dinner with the LaFrance family. (In Kay's vocabulary, "potluck" translates to something along the lines of gourmet dining.) For reservations at Boscobel Cottage, call (318) 325–1550.

You won't want to leave Boscobel, but the time will come when you must. Continue south on U.S. Highway 165 to Columbia.

CALDWELL PARISH

Don't miss the ◆ **Louisiana Art & Folk Center and Museum.** When you reach Columbia, inquire locally for directions to the museum. At the time of my visit, plans were afoot to move from the Pearl Street location because the center's extensive collections required more room. Possible sites were a downtown historic building and the old Martin House, which is north of town and in the process of being restored.

This fascinating facility, a year-round festival in itself, gives you a glimpse of rural life during the early 1900s. You'll see quilts, aprons, clothing, military uniforms, vintage office machines, pump organs, historical documents on Caldwell Parish, an 1859 world atlas, and a rare series of Vietnam photos. The musuem also showcases and sells local arts and crafts.

Vegetables grown on the center's grounds may become home-cooked meals or be presented in glass jars. Canned tomatoes, beets, green beans, pickles, and jellies make splashes of purple, green, red, and gold on scallop-edged pantry shelves. While preserving homegrown foods, the museum's staff also preserves and promotes folk crafts and local history. Typical programs include food preservation, basket-making, crocheting, and tatting. The museum is open Tuesday through Saturday from 9:00 A.M. to 4:30 P.M. year-round. Call (318) 649–6722. Admission is free, although a nominal fee is charged for large groups. Before leaving the museum, ask director Hazel Dailey, Lucille Carpenter, or one of the staff members to give you directions to the **First United Methodist Church.** This picturesque building, painted dark green with white trim, was constructed from plans brought from Europe by a church member and completed in 1911. If time permits, plan a walking tour through the town's hillside cemetery.

32

First United Methodist Church

At this point, you can easily continue south on U.S. Highway 165 to Alexandria and launch an exploration of the state's central section or continue your sightseeing through the state's northeastern corner. While in the Monroe area, plan to meander to nearby Alto for dinner.

RICHLAND PARISH

To reach Alto, take State Route 15 southeast from Monroe (a distance of about 21 miles) or exit Interstate 20 at Start and drive south on State Route 133 then east on State Route 15. ◆ **Bend of the River**, located on the Boeuf River, occupies an old store where W. F. Finley, Jr., and family members serve coleslaw and hush puppies along with that Southern staple, catfish. Looking for a more prosperous livelihood, Mr. Finley said goodbye to farming in 1985 and opened his restaurant, a successful venture that keeps many people busy.

Appetizers include fried dill pickles, stuffed jalapeño peppers, crab claws, onion rings, and seafood gumbo. Also on the menu you'll find crawfish, frog legs, shrimp, crab, oysters, chicken, hamburgers, and steak. Prices are economical to moderate. The restaurant is open only for dinner, and hours are Tuesday through Saturday from 4:30 P.M. until the crowd thins out. Call (318) 248–3840.

If you're near Richland Parish the third Saturday in August, consider taking in the spirited **Southern Pickin' and Grinnin' Festival** held annually in nearby Rayville. After leaving Alto, proceed to Bastrop north of Monroe.

MOREHOUSE PARISH

Across from the Morehouse Parish Courthouse on the town square, you'll see **The Rose Theater,** restored and used for local productions throughout the year. Call (318) 283–0120 for a recording that provides information on current or upcoming events. Tours are available by reservation.

For a light lunch or snack, continue to ◆ **The Johnson House,** located nearby at 409 South Washington. The two-story structure, forest green with cream trim, served as a boardinghouse for teachers during the 1930s and 1940s. In addition to the cafe's fare—salads, sandwiches, desserts, and coffee—The Johnson House offers a gift shop and bed and breakfast accommodations. Standard rates. For more information, call (318) 281–0798.

Before leaving Bastrop, follow U.S. Highway 165 east until it becomes Mer Rouge Road. You'll pass right by the ◆ **Snyder Memorial Museum and Creative Art Center** at 1620 East Madison Street. Housed in a brick building with a roof of red tile, the museum contains furniture from the eighteenth and nineteenth centuries, an Oriental rug in an unusual design, clothing, maps, documents, china, and kitchen utensils. In the living and dining rooms, notice the antique oak furniture with legs carved in a barley-twist design. The museum also features a country store with old-fashioned merchandise, Native American artifacts, historic documents, and monthly art exhibits.

A separate carriage house holds old farm implements, sidesaddles, cotton scales, and a horse-drawn hearse. The grounds offer gardens and picnic facilities, and the museum is open Monday through Friday from 9:00 A.M. until 4:30 P.M. There is no admission charge; call (318) 281–8760.

From Bastrop take Route 133 south until you reach Route 134, which leads east to Epps. Located slightly northeast of Epps (and 15 miles north of Delhi) on Route 577 off Route 134, you'll discover Poverty Point, one of North America's most remarkable archaeological sites.

WEST CARROLL PARISH

If you happen to fly over Louisiana's northeastern corner during winter months when the earth is not camouflaged by foliage, you can see the outline of a great bird with a wingspan of 640 feet. This bird mound was built some three thousand years ago by the advanced people of ◆**Poverty Point.** It boggles the mind to think about the millions of loads of dirt (carried in baskets of animal skin and woven materials and weighing perhaps fifty pounds a load) required to create the site's huge complex of concentric ridges and ceremonial mounds. This tremendous undertaking involved not only tedious labor but a high degree of engineering expertise. In significance this site ranks with England's Stonehenge.

"A whopping total of 1 percent of Poverty Point has been excavated so far," says manager Dennis LaBatt. But that 1 percent tells a remarkable story. When these ridges and mounds were built along Bayou (BYE-yoo) Macon between 1700 and 700 B.C., they were the largest earthworks in the Western Hemisphere. Poverty Point's inhabitants, evidently a bird-revering people, possessed an uncanny degree of astronomical awareness; two of the aisles line up with the summer- and winter-solstice sunsets.

Excavations have uncovered numerous articles of personal adornment, many with bird motifs. Pendants, bangles, and beads of copper, lead, and red jasper appear among the finds. Designs feature various geometric shapes, bird heads, animal claws, locusts, turtles, clam shell replicas, and tiny carved owls. Artifacts also include stone tools, spears, and numerous round clay balls used for cooking.

When LaBatt stages a cooking demonstration to show visitors how the clay balls may have been used, he heats fifty stones and puts them in a pit; he then places venison or fish (wrapped in green leaves) on the heated stones. The food is covered with fifty more stones and allowed to cook slowly.

You can explore the park on foot—it takes between one and two hours to complete the 2.6 mile walking trail—or you can opt for a ride in an open-air tram, which seats thirty adults. The tram tour lasts about forty-five minutes and features stops at Mound A, Mound B, and the terrace ridges.

At the visitors' center, an audiovisual presentation provides some background on Poverty Point, and you'll see displays of artifacts found on the site. There are also picnic facilities here as well as a wooden observation tower that affords an overview of the mounds. If you visit Poverty Point during summer months, you may see an archaeological dig in progress. Several state universities schedule digs during this time, and visitors are welcome to watch the excavations.

Poverty Point's hours are from 9:00 A.M. to 5:00 P.M. seven days a week year-round. Admission is modest; senior citizens and children under twelve are admitted free. Call (318) 926–5492 for more information.

The area surrounding Poverty Point is agricultural country, and the terrain is flat. Along the road you'll see pastureland, crops, cotton gins, and sawmills.

MADISON PARISH

After leaving Poverty Point, head south to Delhi and take U.S. Highway 80 east, watching for a sign to turn right to reach ◆ **Tensas River National Wildlife Refuge** onto a gravel road. To reach the visitors' center, continue south to the end of the road. (When I entered the refuge via a nearby dirt road, five white-tailed deer leaped across the trail in front of me.)

The Tensas (TEN-saw) Refuge's visitors' center is a large rustic building with a rough cedar exterior. Here you can pick up a refuge map and see dioramas and exhibits of birds, mammals, and reptiles indicative of regional wildlife. The building also houses an auditorium where films and slide shows on the refuge's activities may be viewed. The Boardwalk Wildlife Trail, extending about half a mile, takes you to an observation platform. Along the way you may see birds, squirrels, and, yes, snakes.

Tensas is part of a network of refuges that serve as a protected habitat for native wildlife such as the Louisiana black bear. According to one guesstimate about fifty of these bears currently roam the Tensas woods (including the refuge and surrounding forests in Madison Parish).

The Louisiana black bear inspired America's beloved teddy bear. Although the story varies as to locale, it seems that President Theodore Roosevelt, while on a hunting trip to the deep South, wanted to shoot a bear. He once wrote, "I was especially anxious to kill a bear . . . after the fashion of the old southern planters, who for a century past have followed the bear with horse and hound and horn. . . ." Members of Roosevelt's hunting party, knowing of his keen desire to bag a bear, captured a black bear and tied it to a tree—an easy target for the president. Roosevelt's refusal to shoot the helpless animal resulted in much publicity, triggering several editorial cartoons. Soon after the hunting incident, a New York shopkeeper named Morris Michtom came up with the idea of marketing some stuffed toy bears made by his wife Rose. He called them "Teddy's Bears," and the president gave his approval. The Michtoms' cuddly bears became an instant success, and the rest is history.

When I visited the refuge, radios had been placed on fifteen black bears to monitor their activity in a program aimed at preserving and improving their habitat. The radio collars emit signals, which enable park personnel to keep track of the bears' whereabouts.

According to Talbert Williams, a range technician at the refuge, "These small black bears are barely holding their own." Talbert, who was born in a log cabin on the banks of the Tensas River, served over three decades as a wildlife commissioner before going to work for the federal government to "save these woods." He can tell you plenty of local stories, including anecdotes about Ben Lilly, a legendary hunter from these parts.

This habitat also provides food and shelter for many other animals including the bobcat, otter, raccoon, mink, squirrel, woodchuck, wild turkey, barred owl, and pileated woodpecker as well as thousands of migratory birds and waterfowl.

In this bottomland forest you'll also see a great variety of trees—several kinds of oak, three or four specimens of elm, cypress, sweet gum, maple, black locust, honey locust, red haw, and others. There are a few pine and cedar trees, too. Spiky palmetto, muscadine vines, shrubs, and other plants grow here as well.

Deep in the heart of the woods stand the ruins of an old plantation house—about ten handmade-brick pillars (from 10 to 12 feet tall) are all that remain of the former three-story structure. Also hidden in the forest are an old cemetery with eight or nine tombstones and the towering chimney of a pre–Civil War cotton gin.

Primitive canoe launching allows visitors to explore parts of the refuge by boat. Some public hunting is allowed here, but hunters need to familiarize themselves with refuge regulations. Deer hunting permits, which must be requested ahead by writing or phoning, are issued on the basis of drawings. The refuge is open year-round for fishing, but no camping is allowed. As Talbert says, "If you like the natural things, this is the place to come."

The public is welcome to visit the refuge any time of the year. Except for holidays the visitors' center is open Monday through Friday from 8:00 A.M. until 4:00 P.M. From September through December it is also open on Saturday and Sunday from 10:00 A.M. until 4:00 P.M. For further information contact the Refuge Manager, Tensas River National Wildlife Refuge, Route 2, Box 295, Tallulah, LA 71282; the phone number is (318) 574–2664.

After exploring the refuge head northeast to ❖ **Tallulah.** In this area of flat farmland, you'll drive past pecan groves, pastures of grazing cattle, and fields of soybeans, cotton, rice, and wheat.

Tallulah was founded in 1857 and is said to have been named by a traveling railroad engineer in honor of his former sweetheart back home (after he was jilted by a local lady). A bayou winds its way through town and is especially lovely during the holiday season when lights from a series of Christmas trees placed in the water reflect across its surface.

During the early 1900s Tallulah was the site of a government laboratory where experiments were conducted to find a weapon in the war against the boll weevil. By the 1920s aerial crop-dusting techniques were being developed here. In 1924 Delta Airlines (then called Huff Daland Dusters) entered the picture and established the first commercial crop-dusting company.

You can get a good meal at either of Tallulah's two truck-stop restaurants, the **Louisianne** or the **Brushy Bayou** (which serves some of the tastiest catfish strips you'll find anywhere). Visitors can find accommodations at the Southway Inn.

EAST CARROLL PARISH

Traveling north on U.S. Highway 65 takes you to Transylvania, a tiny community with a spooky name. The front window of the ❖**Transylvania General Store** (also known as Norman's Grocery and General Merchandise) features a painting of Dracula and proclaims: "WELCOME TO TRANSYLVANIA. WE'RE ALWAYS GLAD TO HAVE NEW BLOOD IN TOWN!" Adjacent to the store you'll see a small post office and, beyond, a white water tower emblazoned with a black bat.

The store, owned by Norman Chappell, has attracted sight-seers from England, Italy, Iceland, Japan, and even Romania's Transylvania—including a visitor who identified himself as a descendant of Count Dracula.

Besides food, dry goods, and hardware, the Chappells sell life-size rubber bats, skeleton earrings, skull replicas, and about 250 dozen T-shirts a year—some with a Dracula likeness and others with a bat logo. (Be sure to take a peek at the "baby vampire bats" in a lighted box.)

You can get cold soft drinks here and order sandwiches of your choice if you want to brown-bag it. The store, open Monday through Saturday from 6:00 A.M. until 6:30 P.M., closes on Sundays.

After leaving Transylvania, continue north on U.S. Highway 65 (a direct route through the state's northeastern corner to Arkansas) for 10 miles to Lake Providence, home of the ❖**Ole Dutch Bakery.** Located downtown at 208 Lake Street, the bakery offers French, honey whole wheat, and cinnamon breads and other specialties as well. A perennial favorite, the poppy seed bread is made with almond, butter, and vanilla flavorings and topped with a glaze. Owners Kathy and Marlin Wedel also operate an adjoining cafe where you can enjoy lunch; the single daily special might range from a traditional Mennonite recipe to upside-down pizza or cheese enchiladas. The cafe's wooden tables and chairs were made by members of the Wedel's Mennonite congregation. The business actually started in Kathy's kitchen. Her homebaked goods made from traditional Dutch and German recipes proved popular, and the Ole Dutch Bakery opened its doors in 1983. Hours are Tuesday through Friday from 6:30 A.M. until 5:00 P.M. and on Saturday from 6:30 A.M. to 4:00 P.M.

CENTRAL LOUISIANA

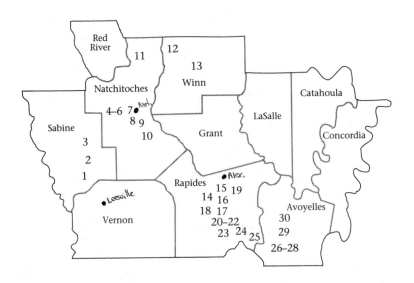

1. Hodges Gardens
2. Fisher
3. Miss-Elaine-E-S
4. Cloutier Townhouse
5. Roque House
6. Martin's Roost
7. Lasyone's Meat Pie Kitchen and Restaurant
8. Beau Fort Plantation
9. Melrose Plantation
10. Bayou Folk Museum
11. Briarwood
12. Mirror Lake Lodge
13. Southern Colonial Bed and Breakfast
14. Kent House
15. Hotel Bentley
16. Alexandria Museum of Art
17. River Oaks Square Arts and Crafts Center
18. Arna Bontemps African-American Museum and Cultural Arts Center
19. Mount Olivet Chapel
20. Lea's Lunchroom
21. Hardy House
22. Old LeCompte School
23. Loyd Hall Plantation
24. Cheneyville Antique Shops
25. Walnut Grove Plantation
26. The Captain's Galley
27. Griffin's Antiques
28. Courtney Gallery of Art
29. Old Corner Antique Shop
30. Tunica-Biloxi Regional Indian Center and Museum

CENTRAL LOUISIANA

SABINE PARISH

About midway between Shreveport and Lake Charles on U.S. Highway 171, you'll find ◈ **Hodges Gardens,** a sight that lures visitors year-round. Created by conservation-minded A. J. Hodges, this forest retreat was once barren land, stripped by timber companies. During the 1940s Hodges replanted thousands of acres with pine trees to bring to pass this outdoor wonderland containing staggered gardens of formal plantings and hillsides strewn with wildflowers. Near the entrance of the main garden area, you'll see a petrified tree—supposedly thousands of years old.

A stone quarry serves as a striking backdrop for moss-covered rocks, waterfalls, and a profusion of wildflowers and other plants. Although featured flowers vary with the season, there's always a lavish display. Acres of daffodils, tulips, and other multicolored bulbs herald spring; camellias, dogwood, and azaleas blazing in reds, corals, and hot pinks confirm the season's arrival. With summer come assorted annuals and thousands of roses bursting into dazzling bloom. Fall furnishes vibrant displays of chrysanthemums—a fantasy in red, pink, purple, yellow, bronze, and white.

Wending your way along pebbled concrete walks that lead past streams and cascading waterfalls, you'll enjoy rainbows of blossoms with sweet aromas. Although the formal gardens are accessible only on foot, you may drive from point to point within the complex. Along the way various panoramic observation points provide breathtaking views. The 4,700 acres of pine forest also serve as home to various birds and animals. You'll see squirrels, wild turkeys, and deer (some seven hundred deer inhabit these woods). Barbados and mouflon sheep and buffalo roam pastures bordering a large lake on the property.

During spring and summer visitors can take cruises in an excursion boat on the 225-acre lake. Rental boats for fishing are also available. Two picnic areas—one nearby equipped with a vending area and rest rooms and the other (without these facilities) in a more remote setting—provide pleasant places for enjoying lunch or a snack. The grounds also offer a conservatory, greenhouses, and a gift shop.

Except Christmas Eve, Christmas Day, and New Year's Day, the gardens are open daily from 8:00 A.M. until sunset; however, the front gate, gift shop, and greenhouses close at 5:00 P.M. Admission is charged. For more information contact Hodges Gardens, P.O. Box 900, Many, LA 71449. The phone number is (318) 586–3523.

Across the road from the entrance to Hodges Gardens is **Toro Hills Golf and Tennis Resort,** where you may want to have dinner or stay overnight. For reservations at Toro Hills Resort, call 1–800–533–5031.

Westward lies Toledo Bend country, an outdoor lover's paradise of some 185,000 acres. Famed for its fine bass fishing, this large recreation area offers a marina, public parks, restaurants, boating facilities, and camping.

To reach ◆ **Fisher,** about a ten-minute drive from Hodges Gardens, follow U.S. Highway 171 north and watch for the turnoff sign. Surrounded by a pine forest and off the beaten path, this hamlet could challenge Garrison Keillor's own Lake Wobegon for the title "The Town That Time Forgot." But therein lies its charm—a quaint and quiet place in today's frenetic world.

When the Louisiana Long Leaf Lumber Company (also known as Four-L) located here in 1899 to harvest the nearby forest of yellow pine, it built Fisher as a base of operations. The town grew into a bustling place with red-dirt streets where mules hauled loads of logs. Made entirely of local lumber, including board sidewalks, each of the town's structures had its own fire hydrant.

Although Fisher's sawmill days ended in 1966 when new owners bought the mill and sold the company houses, you can still see white picket fences, pine cottages, a post office, and an opera house where people stood in line to see movies that cost a dime. There's also an old commissary where folks once shopped, standing a while on the store's long front porch to chat with neighbors.

Joy Phillips applied for grants to restore the commissary, depot, and opera house. She and other village residents are working to preserve the lumber town's past, and Fisher has been placed on the National Register of Historic Districts. Other sites include a caboose painted a fire-engine red with canary-yellow trim, and the Old Fisher Church. Stop by for a snack at the coffee shop, housed in the commissary, and browse through the flea market's displays of antiques, glassware, and other nostalgic merchandise. The flea market's hours are Thursday through Saturday from 9:00 A.M. to 5:00 P.M. and on Sunday from 11:00 A.M. to 6:00 P.M.

Visitors can step back into the village's history each May when Fisher celebrates its heritage with **Sawmill Days,** a festival featuring music, food, entertainment, and a variety of logging and woodworking competitions. For more information on the festival, Fisher's Christmas light display, or the village itself, call (318) 256–6745 or (318) 256–5374.

Continue north on U.S. Highway 171 about 6 miles until you reach Many (MAN-ee). Here, you'll find a friendly place to headquarter at ◆**Miss Elaine-E-S** (miscellaneous), a name Karin and Terry Twedt use to describe their bed and breakfast and other home-based ventures such as antique refinishing and custom framing. Located at 1315 Blake Street in a wooded setting frequented by rabbits, squirrels, and birds, the "contemporary brick and redwood home easily lends itself to entertaining," says Karin. Inside the home, you'll see many antiques, "which are to be enjoyed," she adds, "and ninety percent of them are for sale." You also can purchase gifts, artwork, and craft supplies here. A typical breakfast consists of bacon, eggs, cereal, fresh fruit, and homemade rolls. Rates are standard. For reservations, call (318) 256–6478.

Leaving Many, take Route 6 northeast to Natchitoches Parish.

NATCHITOCHES PARISH

The lovely town of Natchitoches (usually pronounced NAK-a-tish although some old-timers say NAK-a-tosh), which sprang up on the Red River, is now located on the Cane River (actually a lake). The town didn't move—the river did. But perhaps that's why the place retains its historical charm. As Louisiana's oldest town, Natchitoches was a thriving steamboat port that showed promise of growing into a major metropolis, second only to New Orleans, until destiny, in the guise of a spring flood, deemed otherwise. When the Red River carved a new course, Natchitoches was separated from the main body of water and lost its strategic location as a trade center. The shrunken stream left flowing through the old channel was renamed the Cane River. A dam constructed in 1917 created the Cane River Lake, which drifts through the city's heart.

Natchitoches also holds the distinction of being the oldest permanent European settlement in the entire Louisiana Purchase Territory, a vast acreage from which all or parts of fifteen states were carved.

When French Canadian Louis Juchereau de St. Denis (de-NEE) docked here in 1714, he found the Native American Natchitoches (a Caddo tribe) living along the north bank of the Red River. The town takes its name from this tribe, and various translations of the word include chinquapin eaters, chestnut eaters, and pawpaw eaters. St. Denis chose this spot as a trading post with both the Native Americans (the French exchanged guns, knives, and trinkets for furs, bear oil, salt, and such) and the Spanish. To thwart Spanish advances St. Denis established **Fort St. Jean Baptiste.**

You can see a replica of the old French fort with its walls of sharpened logs on the riverfront at Mill Street. The compound, which contains the commandant's house, a small warehouse, chapel, mess hall, and Native American huts, is located near the American Cemetery (where St. Denis and his wife are presumed to be buried). For more information on the fort, call (318) 357–3101.

If you happen to drive through Natchitoches during December, you'll see why it's called the City of Lights. Some 140,000 multicolored lights glow along the downtown riverbank during the Christmas Festival of Lights, an annual event that attracts thousands of sightseers. The movie *Steel Magnolias,* which was filmed in Natchitoches, features some night scenes showing this glittering spectacle. You may want to take a *Steel Magnolias* tour to see some of the locations used in the movie. For more information and a local map, stop by the Natchitoches Parish Tourist Commission at 781 Front Street.

Nearby, in Ducournau (DUKE-er-no) Square on Front Street, you'll find the ◆ **Cloutier Townhouse,** one of the town's three remaining iron-lace buildings. A carriageway from the street leads to a rear brick-paved courtyard, which features an unusual fountain made of plowshares. The stairway on the patio's south side leads to the Cloutier (KLOOCH-er) Townhouse, furnished with early Empire-period antiques, portraits, local art, and artifacts. The home's long gallery overlooks the Cane River Lake. Mother-and-daughter team Conna and Marcie Cloutier own the circa 1835 complex and offer bed-and-breakfast accommodations. Breakfast consists of mini-versions of the traditional Natchitoches meat pie along with different kinds of pastries such as apple brown Betty. Rates are standard to moderate. Call (318) 352–5242.

You'll enjoy strolling through the Historic District with its charming eighteenth- and nineteenth-century houses. Many of the town's old homes feature filigreed balconies of "frozen lace" similar to those in New Orleans. Natchitoches is known as the New Orleans of the North, and its historic district has been designated a National Historic Landmark. Running north and south, the Cane River parallels the town's main street, which has three names: It's called Jefferson Street on the south end near Northwestern State University, turns into Front Street in the downtown area, and then becomes Washington Street on the north side.

Along the town's picturesque brick-paved Front Street, you'll pass many antebellum structures in the original downtown area. At the 1843 Hughes Building, be sure to notice the courtyard with its ornate spiral staircase of cast iron.

To continue your exploration you can park down by the riverside, just below Front Street, to see the ◆ **Roque House.** Located on the bank of Cane River Lake, the Roque (rock) House dates from the 1790s. Originally built as a residence at nearby Isle Brevelle, the French Colonial structure of hand-hewn cypress was moved to its present site during the 1960s. The restored wood-shingled cottage is especially noted for its *bousillage* (BOO-see-ahj) construction. *Bousillage,* which was used in a number of the state's French Colonial buildings, was made by boiling Spanish moss and combining it with mud and hair scraped from animal hide. When packed between wooden wall posts, the procedure was known as *bousillage entre poteaux.* Covered with plaster (sometimes made with lime and deer hair), this mixture provided good insulation.

Natchitoches offers a number of other attractions such as the Old Courthouse and the Immaculate Conception Catholic Church, both located on Second and Church streets, and also the Trinity Parish Church at Second and Trudeau streets.

A comfortable place to make your base (or nest) in Natchitoches is ◆ **Martin's Roost,** only ten minutes from the Histor-

Roque House

ical District. Owned by Vicki and Ronald Martin, the home is located at 1735½ Washington Street on the edge of town. Perched on a bluff overlooking a dry bed where the Red River once flowed and surrounded by pastures and wooded areas, this contemporary home features a large deck and pool. The bed and breakfast facility offers two guest rooms, each with private bath. One bedroom opens onto a courtyard complete with bubbling fountain—an ideal spot for bird-watching.

Martin's Roost houses a treasury of crafts including Ron's unique birdhouses, which he sometimes exhibits when he accompanies Vicki to art and craft shows. Several of Vicki's award-winning original counted cross-stitch designs depict Natchitoches landmarks, and you'll see some of her creations on the walls. You can enjoy a tour—in miniature—of local plantations because the Martins have made Lilliputian-sized replicas of a number of nearby historic buildings. They also collaborate on built-to-scale plantation-style dollhouses.

Vicki provides plenty of tips and information on where to go and what to do while in the area. She keeps brochures, maps, and local restaurant menus on hand and also offers a personalized tour service to local sites by the hour, half-day, or day.

You can anticipate a feast here. A menu on the kitchen's blackboard might read HOUSE BREAKFAST: BROILED GRAPEFRUIT, BOUILLON,

47

SWEET ROLLS, BAKED HAM-CHEESE OMELET, HOLLYWOOD BILL'S BROWN BREAD, GOUMI BERRY AND PLUM JELLIES, COFFEE, TEA, AND JUICE.

To elaborate on Vicki's menu, she often starts breakfast with her luscious artichoke-and-mushroom soup, an original recipe that falls in the gourmet category. As for her homemade jellies, she sometimes serves mayhaw jelly, made from a wild fruit found in river bottomlands and swamps. Vicki's goumi (GOOM-me) berry jelly comes from the mayhaw's almost extinct dryland cousin, a bush that produces colorful berries resembling jelly-beans. Hollywood Bill's Brown Bread is a popular item on the menu. The recipe, which Vicki will share with you, comes from *Steel Magnolias'* set decorator.

Rates are standard. If you make reservations ahead, you can also have dinner here; prices are reasonable. For bed and break-fast accommodations, call (318) 352–9215.

Don't leave Natchitoches without stopping by ❧ **Lasyone's Meat Pie Kitchen and Restaurant,** located at 622 Second Street. Meat pies, the featured specialty, resemble fried fruit pies except for the filling. To make his famous creations, James Lasy-one (lassie-OWN) uses a combination of pork and ground beef with onions and spices. The slowly cooked meat is later thick-ened with a *roux* (a sauce of flour and fat that adds flavor and body) and chilled overnight. At serving time a dollop of the mix-ture is dropped on a circle of dough; after the crust is folded over and crimped on the edges, the pie is ready to fry.

A former grocer, Mr. Lasyone has been in the restaurant busi-ness more than twenty years and is assisted by his wife, Jo Ann, and other family members. The restaurateur remembers when men pushed metal carts through the streets of Natchitoches, sell-ing "hotta-meat-pies."

Order a meat pie with dirty rice (the name given to the dark-stained version cooked with chicken giblets) and a green salad. For dessert you'll want to try another house specialty, Cane River cream pie. The restaurant offers a complete menu and features daily luncheon specials, such as veal tips, catfish, or chicken breast. Rates are economical. Hours are Monday through Saturday from 7:00 A.M. to 7:00 P.M. Call (318) 352–3353.

Allow some time for driving through the fertile plantation coun-try surrounding Natchitoches, where you'll see pecan groves and fields of soybeans and cotton. You'll also want to visit one or more of the many nearby plantation homes for which Cane River country is famous, but be sure to call before you go because operating hours change. If possible schedule an afternoon visit to ◆ **Beau Fort Plantation,** an antebellum home located 10 miles south of town on Route 119, about halfway between Natchitoches and Melrose Plantation. An avenue of live oaks leads to the house, which occupies the grounds where historic Fort Charles stood during the 1760s. A wide cottage-style structure of Creole architecture dating from about 1790, the house features an 84-foot front gallery. Constructed of hand-hewn cypress timbers and *bousillage* walls, the home is listed on the National Register of Historic Places.

Over the dining-room table, you'll see a punkah (also called a "shoo fly") which was installed when the house was built. Be sure to notice the plantation scenes depicted on the library's wallpaper. Among the home's many interesting antiques are a rosewood plantation desk dating from 1790 and, in the Stranger's Room, a 1790 bed with hand-carved posts in a pineapple and acanthus leaf pattern. A brick and antique ironwork fence encloses a lovely rear garden.

Beau Fort is open from 1:00 to 4:00 P.M. daily except Christmas Day, New Year's Day, Thanksgiving, and Independence Day (July 4). Admission is modest. For more information call (318) 352–5340 or (318) 352–9580.

Don't miss ◆**Melrose Plantation,** 2 miles east of Route 1 at the junction of Routes 493 and 119. Your guide will tell you the legend of the remarkable Marie Thérèse Coincoin, a freed slave who obtained a land grant from the Spanish colonial authorities and, with the help of her sons, established and operated what is now Melrose Plantation.

You'll see the Yucca House, Marie Thérèse's original two-room cypress-timbered home built in 1796 and the African House, supposedly the only original Congolike architecture still standing in the United States. Other plantation buildings include the white clapboard Big House built in 1833 by Marie Thérèse's grandson, the Weaving House, the Bindery, Ghana House, and the Writer's Cabin. Also on the grounds is the cabin home of former Melrose cook, Clementine Hunter, whose colorful and charming murals cover the upstairs walls of the African House.

At one time Melrose was one of the country's largest pecan orchards. John Henry purchased the plantation in 1898, and his wife restored Melrose and turned it into a renowned retreat for artists and writers. Among the many writers who accepted the hospitality of Miss Cammie (Mrs. Henry) were François Mignon, Erskine Caldwell, Lyle Saxon, and Caroline Dormon.

Melrose, which closes on all major holidays, is open daily from noon to 4:00 P.M. Admission is modest; call (318) 379–0055 or (318) 379–2431.

Approximately 25 miles south of Natchitoches just off Route 1 on Route 495, you'll find the ◆ **Bayou Folk Museum.** This building, which dates from the early 1800s, is located on Main Street in the charming village of Cloutierville (KLOOCH-er-vil). The only place to park is on the narrow street in front of the museum; local traffic, however, tends to be light.

Constructed of slave-made brick, cypress mortised with square wooden pegs, and *bousillage,* the raised-cottage style structure contains four fireplaces that share a single chimney. An exterior staircase leads to the second floor, which served as the living area.

Author Kate Chopin lived in this house with her husband and six children from 1879 until 1884. In the downstairs entrance room, you'll see a showcase featuring an original edition of *Bayou Folk,* a collection of Mrs. Chopin's short stories about Creole life in which she uses Cane River country as a setting. Portraits of the author and her family, along with a number of their possessions including silverware and Mrs. Chopin's sidesaddle, are also on display.

Other rooms feature various collections of jewelry, china, glass, sewing machines, school desks, early phonographs, oak iceboxes, Civil War firearms, and antique furniture. On the upstairs rear porch, you'll see an unusual old sharpshooter coffin.

The museum complex also contains a blacksmith shop, a mule-operated sugar cane mill, and a country doctor's office, furnished with medical equipment and instruments once used by plantation doctors. Except for major holidays, the Bayou Folk Museum is open Monday through Saturday from 10:00 A.M. to 5:00 P.M. and from 1:00 to 5:00 P.M. on Sunday. Admission is modest. Call (318) 379–2233 for more information.

If time permits drive south along Route 1, where you'll see acres of pecan groves. One of Louisiana's oldest and largest pecan producers, **Litta Eva Plantation** (which takes its name from the plantation in *Uncle Tom's Cabin*) is nearby. Several pecan processing plants dot the roadside in this area. In season you can stop and buy whole or shelled pecans, roasted pecans, candies made with pecans, and other nutty delights.

Afterward you can either drive on to Alexandria, the state's crossroads, or head north of Natchitoches to take in some interesting sites in that direction.

Taking the northern option, you can retrace your route to Natchitoches or get on U.S. Highway 71 north for a visit to ◆ **Briarwood** in the northwest corner of Natchitoches Parish. This wonderful wooded area, some 19 miles north of Campti, is located just off Route 9, north of Readhimer and 2 miles south of Saline. (Saline is especially noted for its fine watermelons, so you may want to stop and buy one if you pass this way during summer months.) Briarwood, a wild garden definitely off the beaten path, will especially delight botanists and bird-watchers. A rustic sign suspended over a wooden gate marks the entrance to this 125-acre nature preserve, once the home of Caroline Dormon, America's first woman to be employed in forestry.

A pioneer conservationist, Miss Dormon played a major role in establishing Louisiana's Kisatchie National Forest, which extends over seven parishes and covers 600,000 acres. Also known internationally for her work as a naturalist, Miss Dormon described and painted rare native species of plants. Her books *Flowers Native to the Deep South* and *Wild Flowers of Louisiana* are both botany classics.

Briarwood boasts Louisiana's largest collection of plants native to the southeast, where spring might bring spectacular shows of pink dogwoods, white pompons, crabapples, pale pink native azaleas, and mottled-green trilliums. The nature preserve is also home to a woodland iris garden and six different species of pitcher plants.

Briarwood's curators Jessie and Richard Johnson, who knew "Miss Carrie" personally, will welcome you to this serene retreat, which can be explored on foot or by golf cart. Richard, who calls Briarwood a "place of renewal, a balm for the soul," will show you Miss Carrie's former log cabin home, deep in the woods. Now a museum, the house contains furniture, household items, and original illustrations from one of the naturalist's books. Be sure to spend a few minutes looking through the scrapbooks where you'll see some of Miss Carrie's correspondence. One note to a friend reads: "That everlastin' bird book is out at last! I'm bound to say I think it's a darlin'—even if I am its mama!"

Surrounding the cabin you'll see many giant trees, including a longleaf pine possibly three centuries old, known as Grandpappy. Nearby are tulip and sourwood trees, big-leafed magnolias, and native sasanquas—fall-blooming camellias with delicate blossoms and handsome dark foliage.

A trail winds past a pond and through tall pines, mountain laurel, and wild ginger to a one-room cabin on a gentle knoll even farther back in the forest. The simply-furnished log house, called Three Pines Cabin, served as Miss Carrie's retreat for writing and painting when too many visitors found their way to Briarwood. "This was her hideaway," Jessie says, "when the world beat a path to her door."

As a memento of your visit to Briarwood, Jessie may break off some vines of bittersweet (with golden-brown buds that later burst into red berries), which you can take home and tuck in a flower arrangement.

Even though Briarwood does not advertise, some two thousand visitors discover it each year. The nature preserve is open to the public every weekend in March, April, May, August, and November. Hours are from 9:00 A.M. to 5:00 P.M. on Saturday and from noon to 5:00 P.M. on Sunday. Tours at other times may be arranged by appointment. Admission is charged. For more information, call (318) 576–3379.

If you're ready for a hearty meal after your trek through the woods, head for nearby Winn Parish.

Winn Parish

To reach ◆**Mirror Lake Lodge,** located in the northwestern tip of Winn Parish, take Route 126 from Readhimer and travel about 2 miles east. You should see the turnoff for the lodge on the left. If you pass Route 1233, which enters Route 126 from the right, you've gone too far. To further pinpoint the lodge's location, Bienville Parish is "just a fish-flop north," according to members of the Carpenter clan, who run this "old country inn rolled in cornmeal." The restaurant, which serves some of the state's best catfish, stands on a hill overlooking a man-made lake (originally called Blewers Pond) fed by fifteen springs. A friend of the Blewers, singer Hank Williams visited their home here, now Mirror Lake Lodge, and the house is said to have inspired his song "Mansion on the Hill."

The lodge, which can seat up to two hundred persons, is a popular spot for class and family reunions. Alternating red and blue checkered oilcloth covers the tables. Restaurant owner D. C. Carpenter sometimes entertains guests, particularly the Sunday luncheon crowd, with his piano music, which ranges from "old-timey and gospel to country and western," says cook Betty Carpenter. Betty, Jimmy, Sonya, and other family members help D. C. run the restaurant. Even though Mirror Lake Lodge is a word-of-mouth kind of place that attracts lots of local folks, the Carpenters have a faithful following from a radius of 150 miles.

The restaurant serves catfish with hush puppies, french fries, and coleslaw. You also can order oysters, shrimp, steak, or chicken, and all portions are generous. Prices are economical to moderate.

Mirror Lake Lodge does not serve alcohol, and no credit cards are accepted. Closed on Mondays, the restaurant's hours are from 4:00 to 10:00 P.M. on Tuesday, Wednesday, and Thursday. Friday and Saturday hours are from 10:00 A.M. to 10:00 P.M. and on Sunday the restaurant is open from 10:00 A.M. to 4:00 P.M. For more information contact Mirror Lake Lodge, Route 1, Box 134, Saline, LA 71010, or call (318) 576–3688.

Afterward head toward Winnfield, the birthplace of Huey P. Long, O. K. Allen, and Earl K. Long, all former governors of Louisiana. Driving through the downtown area, be sure to notice the old **Winnfield Hotel,** used in the filming of *Blaze*—a movie about Louisiana politics in which Paul Newman portrayed Governor Earl K. Long.

While in Winnfield, a pleasant place to stay overnight is ◆**Southern Colonial Bed and Breakfast,** located at 801 East Main Street. The towering two-story house dates from about 1908, and owners Judy and John Posey will welcome you to their home, which features an inviting front porch and seven fireplaces. The Poseys occupy the downstairs portion. The second floor, reserved for overnight visitors, features a common parlor and large guest rooms with some interesting antiques. Amenities include cable television, phones, coffee, and wake-up alarms. Guests can enjoy refreshments on the balcony or on the large porch, shaded by an ancient oak tree. To start the day one can opt for a continental breakfast included in the standard rate or a traditional Southern breakfast for an extra fee. Call (318) 628–6087.

A short stroll from the Poseys' home, you'll find the **Earl K. Long State Commemorative Area.** Established in honor of Louisiana's first three-term governor, the one-acre park features a symmetrical design and lovely landscaping. An 8-foot bronze statue, dedicated on July 4, 1963, stands as a memorial to Earl Kemp Long, younger brother of Huey Long. A hedged circular sidewalk leads to a pavilion, a pleasant spot for a picnic.

From Winnfield, take U.S. Highway 167 south to Alexandria.

RAPIDES PARISH

Known as a crossroads city, Alexandria marks the state's geographic center. The parish seat of Rapides (ra-PEEDS), Alexandria lost most of its buildings and records in 1864 when the Yankees set fire to the city during the Civil War. Another disaster occurred with the flood of 1866. The Red River separates Alexandria from her sister city, Pineville.

Arriving in Alexandria on Route 28, you'll come to a traffic circle. Go south on Route 71 for about a mile and turn right on Route 496 to reach ◆**Kent House** at 3601 Bayou Rapides Road. Believed to be Central Louisiana's oldest existing building (one of few area structures to survive the Civil War), the home dates from about 1796. Kent House, which stands on brick pillars, exemplifies the classic Louisiana style of French and Spanish Colonial architecture. An elevated construction protected buildings from floods and dampness.

Now restored, the house was moved to its present location from the original site, six blocks away. Kent House serves as a museum where visitors may see seven period rooms filled with Empire, Sheraton, and Federal furniture, authentic documents dealing with land transfers, and many interesting decorative items.

The four-acre complex also contains slave quarters, a notched-log carriage house, a barn, a blacksmith shop, and gardens. You'll see a detached kitchen and milk house along with a collection of early nineteenth-century cooking utensils. From October through April open-hearth cooking demonstrations are given each Wednesday between 9:00 A.M. and 2:00 P.M. Prepared foods might include cornbread, chicken, corn soup, lima beans, and pie. Admission is modest. Kent House is open from 9:00 A.M. to 5:00 P.M. every day except on Sunday when the hours are from 1:00 to 5:00 P.M. Call (318) 487–5998.

Don't miss ❖ **Hotel Bentley,** sometimes called the Biltmore of the Bayou or the Waldorf of the Red River. Located at 200 Desoto Street, the hotel dates from 1908. According to local legend, lumber baron Joseph A. Bentley (originally from Pennsylvania), dressed in his work clothes, was refused service at an Alexandria hotel. He then proceeded to erect his own grand establishment, Hotel Bentley, where he lived until his death in 1939.

Listed on the National Register of Historic Places, the hotel serves as a fine example of turn-of-the-century Renaissance Revival architecture. The large lobby's classic Ionic columns flank a grand staircase leading to the mezzanine, where north and south wings feature striking skylights of stained glass. You can enjoy breakfast, lunch, or dinner at the Bentley Restaurant on the substreet level.

Be sure to stop by the Mirror Room. Decorated in red, black, and silver, the room features a mirrored ceiling, black marble dance floor, and seven imported hand-painted windows depicting German pub figures.

With five major military camps nearby, Central Louisiana served as the hub of a nine-state area for training military personnel during World War II. It is said that some strategies for World War II battles were mapped out at Hotel Bentley, sometimes on napkins in the Mirror Room. Many troop commanders and other eminent military figures either lived at Hotel Bentley or visited during this period. The hotel's guest register records such names as Major General George Patton, General George C. Marshall, General Matthew B. Ridgway, Lieutenant Colonel Omar Bradley, Colonel Dwight Eisenhower, and Lieutenant Henry Kissinger.

In the hotel's Venetian Room, couples danced to the music of Tommy Dorsey and many of the era's big bands. With Central Louisiana as the base for thousands of troops being sent overseas, the hotel became a center for family and friends of the military.

55

When every hotel room was filled, the management handed out pillows and blankets to visitors, who camped in the lobby.

For reservations, call (318) 448–9600 or 1–800–356–6835.

From the Bentley it's a short walk to the ◆ **Alexandria Museum of Art** at 933 Main Street. You may want to take your car, however, to save time afterward. The museum occupies the original Rapides Bank building, which dates from 1898, the first major building to appear after twin disasters of fire and flood in the 1860s. The facility features a fine collection of modern and contemporary works as well as Louisiana folk arts and traveling exhibits. The museum, which also sponsors educational and interpretive programs, is open Monday through Friday from 9:00 A.M. to 5:00 P.M. Saturday hours are from 10:00 A.M. to 4:00 P.M. Admission fee is nominal; call (318) 443–3458.

Continue to nearby ◆ **River Oaks Square Arts and Crafts Center** at 1330 Main Street. This lovely Queen Anne–style house, the original residence of the Bolton family, was given to the city by Peggy Bolton to be used for the arts. Thirty-four local artists now work at the center, and you can watch creativity in action as painters, weavers, and sculptors practice their callings— you can peek over artist Clyde Downs's shoulder as he paints an expressionistic landscape or watch Beverly Price stitch a quilt from one of her original designs. In addition to showcasing artists at work, the center also offers classes and workshops in drawing, watercolor, print making, weaving, sculpture, and collage for both children and adults.

River Oaks Square is open Monday through Friday from 10:00 A.M. to 4:00 P.M. Besides browsing, you can also buy unique works of art. There is no admission charge; call (318) 473–2670.

A few steps behind River Oaks Square, you'll find the ◆ **Arna Bontemps African-American Museum and Cultural Arts Center** at 1327 Third Street. Bontemps, a member of the Harlem Renaissance, authored novels, poetry, plays, histories, folklore collections, biographies, and children's literature. Housed in the circa 1890 home where Bontemps was born in 1902, the museum contains the author's typewriter, books, letters, and memorabilia such as photographs of Louis Armstrong, Sidney Poitier, and other entertainers and arts figures. In addition to preserving a literary legacy, Bontemps's childhood home serves as a setting for traveling exhibits, area art displays, and writing classes for local youngsters. The center also showcases the Hall of Fame collection originally kept at LSU's Alexandria branch. Except for major holidays, hours are Tuesday through Saturday from 10:00 A.M. to 4:00 P.M. Call (318) 449–5000 or (318) 442–0095 for more information. A nominal donation is requested.

Afterward, drive back toward the Hotel Bentley and turn right to cross the bridge that spans the Red River. This takes you to Pineville's Main Street. You'll soon see a cemetery on the left and then ✜**Mount Olivet Chapel.** Built in 1854, the church was dedicated by Bishop Leonidas Polk, who later "buckled sword over gown" to became a Confederate general. The picturesque chapel survived the Civil War probably because it served as a headquarters for the Union Army.

The Gothic Revival structure, which features some Tiffany windows, was designed by Richard Upjohn, the architect of New York's Trinity Church. Except for its oak floor, the chapel is constructed entirely of native pinewood. Although the building is kept locked, the instructions for getting a key are posted on the side door. Take some time to explore the surrounding cemetery with tombstone dates as early as 1824 still discernible.

Military buffs may want to visit the **Alexandria National Cemetery** at 209 Shamrock Avenue, also in Pineville. This cemetery, an art gallery in stone, contains graves from the Civil War, Spanish-American War, and both World Wars.

After visiting Pineville take U.S. Highway 71 south to Lecompte, about 12 miles south of Alexandria. Here you'll find ✜**Lea's Lunchroom,** a country-style cafe that dishes up hearty Southern cooking. Lea Johnson established this popular eatery in 1928. At age 93, Mr. Lea, as he is fondly known, appeared on the "Tonight Show" and swapped quips with Johnny Carson, and you can watch a videotape of the program while here. Even though the restaurant is now operated by his daughter, Ann Johnson, Mr. Lea, who is quite an entertainer, pays regular visits and fraternizes with the customers.

Mr. Lea believes in fast service and objects to written menus because "they take too much time." At Lea's the server recites the menu, which might feature red beans and sausage with rice and crackling cornbread or a choice of fried fish, beef tips, or ham along with turnip greens, sweet potatoes, and coconut pudding. Rates are economical. Milk is served in frosted glasses, and you can have a demitasse of coffee after your meal. "Three cups of that South Louisiana coffee will kill you," Mr. Lea warns. The restaurant is famous for its hams baked in dough and homemade pies made from secret family recipes. The staff makes about 71,000 pies a year, including apple, pecan, banana cream, cherry, blueberry, blackberry, lemon, chocolate, and coconut.

The restaurant also offers a large selection of cookbooks such as *My Favorite Recipes,* compiled by Jessie V. Chop, who includes her comments for successful versions of such dishes as Louisiana red beans and rice, fried chicken, "fist" biscuits, and fig preserves. Lea's hours are from 7:00 A.M. to 7 P.M. Except for major holidays, the restaurant is open seven days a week. Call (318) 776–5178.

While in Lecompte, you may want to headquarter at ◈ **Hardy House,** a lovely home at 1414 Weems. Owner Ann Johnson enjoys rescuing historic structures and spent a year and a half restoring the 1888 home. Now a bed and breakfast furnished with fine antiques and accent pieces, this exquisite Victorian restoration with its color scheme in rich jewel tones showcases Ann's decorating talents and art background. The honeymoon suite features a double-sized footed tub with brass fixtures. Overnight guests can opt for a home-cooked breakfast at Hardy House or eat at nearby Lea's. Rates are standard to moderate. Call Lea's at (318) 776–5178 for reservations and specific directions.

Lea's hours are from 7:00 A.M. to 7:00 P.M. Tuesday through Sunday. The restaurant closes on Monday. Call (318) 776–5178.

Lecompte (le-COUNT) was named after an 1850s record-breaking racehorse from a local plantation. Before a sign painter inadvertently inserted a *P,* the place was Lecomte. While in town stop by the ◈ **Old Lecompte School,** which dates from 1924. Local citizens recently waged a campaign to resurrect their old school—where shouts of students and chiming class bells had not been heard for over two decades—and won an award from the state for their success story. Now a community center, the large building houses a museum, dining room, public library, meeting rooms, gymnasium, and auditorium.

According to Bill King, chairman of the committee to save the school, the remarkable thing about this project is that it was entirely a community effort. All money came from private donations, and local people volunteered their talents to renovate the structure. The building's distinctive historical features, including the auditorium's ornate plasterwork and balcony railing, have been preserved. The end result is a fine multipurpose facility that holds a treasury of memories for generations of former students.

Before leaving this area you may want to drive through the surrounding countryside. Some two hundred nurseries are located in the nearby Lecompte–Forest Hill area. Along **Nursery Row** you'll find landscaping bargains in a variety of shrubs, trees, and plants, including ornamental and exotic plants. Although the nurseries supply commercial markets, most will accommodate drop-in retail customers. After your drive take U.S. Highway 71 south to Cheneyville.

To reach ◆ **Loyd Hall Plantation,** follow U.S. Highway 167, off U.S. Highway 71 near Cheneyville. Anne and Frank Fitzgerald will welcome you to their lovely three-story antebellum home, which dates from 1810. This classic white-columned plantation house features original pine-heart flooring, cypress woodwork, and medallioned ceilings.

Loyd Hall Plantation

You'll enjoy seeing the elegant furnishings and learning about the house's history. According to a New Orleans psychic, three resident ghosts prowl the huge rooms at Loyd Hall, and you'll hear some interesting stories about them. Supposedly a violinist appears at midnight on the second-floor gallery and plays sad songs. When visitors ask Anne if she's heard the ghostly tunes, she usually answers that after her exhausting day, she's sound asleep by midnight. (When I visited, I was asleep by that time, too. I did go outside earlier, however, to snap a few night photos of the mansion. The resulting pictures contained some eerie white streaks, which I attributed to my photography—but who knows?) If you visit Loyd Hall, you won't have to worry about the ghosts because they live in the big house, and overnight guests sleep in the adjacent cypress country cottage.

Visitors to the plantation can see various agricultural operations in action. Cotton, corn, soybeans, and cattle are raised here. "We let our guests gather pecans and pick cotton," Anne notes. "People are intrigued with cotton." One visitor took a cotton-seed back to her home in Paris, planted it in a pot on her balcony, and nourishes it like a house plant.

The mansion is open for luncheons, receptions, and tours. In addition to the main house, guided tours include a museum, which is furnished with vintage items, and an antique and gift shop. Tour hours are from 10:00 A.M. to 4:00 P.M. Tuesday through Saturday and from 1:00 to 4:00 P.M. on Sunday. For reservations, call 1–800–749–1928 or (318) 776–5641. Rates are moderate.

If you enjoy antiquing expeditions, you'll find both Cheneyville and the nearby town of Bunkie fertile territory. Don't miss the ◆Cheneyville Antique Shops along U.S. Highway 71. Entering Cheneyville, you'll spot Bob Cox's Antiques on a downtown corner at Scott Street. The two-story red brick shop features a fine selection of Victorian and Empire period pieces. You'll see handsome dining room tables, secretaries, and four-poster beds in mahogany, rosewood, and walnut. A high wheeler (an antique bicycle with a large front wheel and small back wheel) hangs from the ceiling, and minature cotton bales dot shelves and tables. Bob, who carries a line of paintings and various decorative accessories, also provides helpful hints on refinishing furniture. If you discover an antique you can't live without, Bob will ship it to your home. Call (318) 279–2376.

Continue your exploration at nearby **Daddy Sam's, Sadler's A to Z, Bygone Days,** and **Jackie's Antiques,** which offer a variety of choice Louisiana and European furnishings and collectibles. Shop hours generally run from 10:00 A.M. to 5:00 P.M. Monday through Saturday and from 1:00 to 5:00 P.M. on Sunday. Call (318) 279–2155 or (318) 279–2375.

Before leaving Cheneyville, consider stopping by **Producer's Mutual Cotton Gin** (across from Jackie's Antiques) to learn about cotton production in its various stages. Tours are conducted all year, but the most exciting time to visit is during ginning season, usually September (although it can start as early as mid-August) through November when the facility runs twenty-four hours a day. During this time, visitors can observe a working gin in action. Except for Thursday (payroll day), visitors are welcome weekdays from 9:00 A.M. to 3:00 P.M. Admission is free. Call (318) 279–2145.

Located off U.S. Highway 71, 2 miles southeast of Cheneyville near Bayou Boeuf, you'll find ◆**Walnut Grove Plantation.** The impressive Tudor-style home was once part of a 4,000-acre plantation with an assortment of outbuildings including a sawmill, cotton gin, sugar mill, and barns. The house, built between 1835 and 1848, still contains many of its original furnishings. You'll enjoy strolling along the garden's restored brick walks with a backdrop of magnolias and venerable oak trees.

Walnut Grove, which specializes in weddings and receptions, is open for tours Tuesday through Saturday from 10:00 A.M. to 4:00 P.M. Sunday hours are from 1:00 to 4:00 P.M. Admission is modest. The plantation also offers bed and breakfast accommodations at nearby Sunniside Cottage and Buttercup House where the rates are moderate to deluxe. For more information call (318) 279–2203.

After visiting Walnut Grove, head south on U.S. Highway 71 to Bunkie.

AVOYELLES PARISH

Here in Avoyelles Parish, named for a Native American tribe, you'll dip into Cajun territory. Even without a map you can tell when you get to **Acadiana**—the language changes, the food becomes spicy, and the coffee gets strong.

Don't pass through Bunkie without stopping at ◆**The Captain's Galley.** Located on U.S. Highway 71 north and Ebony

61

Road on the town's north side, the restaurant specializes in Louisiana boiled crawfish. You'll also find excellent seafood and steaks here. Start with the scrumptious shrimp-crab puffs served with a creamy horseradish sauce. Then try the Captain's special seafood platter with shrimp, oysters, stuffed crab, catfish, and other fresh Gulf Coast delicacies. Another popular entrée, the shrimp and crabmeat *au gratin,* comes with a green salad and French bread. Don't leave the restaurant without trying one of the dessert specialties such as cheesecake with white chocolate topping or old-fashioned bread pudding with warm rum sauce.

The Ferguson family operates The Captain's Galley, which is open from 11:00 A.M. to 2:00 P.M. Monday through Friday and from 5:00 to 9:00 P.M. Tuesday through Saturday. It is closed Sunday. Call (318) 346–2403.

At **Griffin's Antiques,** on the corner of Church and Main streets, you'll see a large selection of stained-glass windows. Owner Toni Griffin, assisted by her daughter Doris Maillet, will show you a selection of outstanding antiques including many signed Louisiana pieces. The shop carries such items as mahogany marble-topped dressers and washstands, rosewood parlor tables, beds, consoles, cupboards, Meissen candelabra, fine china, silver and, cut crystal. Hours are Tuesday through Saturday from 9:00 A.M. to 5:00 P.M. or by appointment. Call (318) 346–2806 or (318) 346–6275.

Before leaving Bunkie, be sure to stop by the ◆ **Courtney Gallery of Art** at 400 Walnut Street, one block off Main Street. After a sojourn in Georgia, Juanita Courtney returned to her hometown and, with husband Kent, opened an art gallery. A professional painter for some thirty years, Juanita's subject matter ranges from landscapes, house portraits, and still life to barnyard animals, wild animals, and pet portraits. Her original oils and watercolors, along with a large selection of prints, may be purchased here.

Besides his Scottish tam, Kent wears a number of figurative hats—he has been a radio commentator, newspaper writer, editor, publisher, and poet. Kent's poems of consolation, motivation, and inspiration, rendered in calligraphy and embellished with artwork, make lovely wall hangings and are available matted and/or framed. The gallery also carries an assortment of gifts such as pottery, sculpture, and decorative decoys. You can visit the

Courtneys during their usual business hours of 10:00 A.M. to 5:00 P.M. Call (318) 346-9966 or (318) 346-9964.

After exploring Bunkie, head northeast about 11 miles to Hessmer where you'll be greeted by a host of barnyard sounds when you visit Howard Ducote's ❖ **Old Corner Antique Shop.** Here in a former dairy barn, Howard houses an enormous collection of armoires, marble-topped tables, slipper chairs, cupboards, beds, mantels, mirrors, and china. Chickens, guineas, ducks, geese, and turkeys strut about in a large pen behind the barn. You'll probably find Howard wearing a leather apron, busy at work refinishing an antique piece. For more information on his inventory and specific directions, call his shop at (318) 563–8247.

While in the area, you may want to swing about 5 miles east to Mansura where Howard's mother, Lena Ducote, lives at 440 Leglise Street. In her shop, housed in an old bank building adjacent to her home, Mrs. Ducote carries a selection of dolls and dishes along with some antique furnishings. She also offers caning and furniture refinishing services. Although Mrs. Ducote does not keep regular business hours, she often opens her shop by request.

Head northeast to Marksville. Located one-half mile south of town, just off Route 1 south, you'll find the ❖ **Tunica-Biloxi Regional Indian Center and Museum.** This 134-acre Indian reservation features a pyramidlike museum, which contains a collection of artifacts valued at $5 million—the famed **Tunica Treasure.** Anthropologist William Day, who serves as museum director and assistant tribal planner, will fill you in on the fascinating history of this extraordinary collection of Indian and European artifacts.

Taken from Tunica Indian burial sites by pot hunters, these fruits of colonial entrepreneurship have finally been returned to the Tunica tribe (after a long legal battle) and are appropriately housed in a structure shaped like a temple mound. You'll see Native American and European artifacts dating from 1731 to 1764, which the Tunicas amassed in transactions with the French, Spanish, English, and other Native Americans during the state's colonial period. Among the many colorful exhibits are displays of Indian pottery, shell beads, basketry, almost 400 brass and copper kettles, 166 flintlock muskets, several hundred pieces of European ceramics, 200,000 beads of European manufacture, and jewelry made from Spanish silver coins.

Pottery, baskets, beadwork, and other Native American crafts are sold here. The Tunica-Biloxi Museum is open Tuesday through Saturday from 8:00 A.M. to 4:30 P.M. Admission is modest. Call (318) 253–8174.

Adjacent to the town of Marksville and about a mile or so from the reservation, you'll find the Marksville State Commemorative Area. Due to a lack of funding, the state-owned museum is presently closed; however, you can still see six prehistoric **Indian mounds** as well as encircling earthworks ranging from 4 to 6 feet tall. Marksville's Indian civilization, contemporaneous with Ohio's Hopewell culture, flourished here some 2,000 years ago. Situated on a bluff, the Marksville site overlooks Old River.

SOUTHWEST LOUISIANA

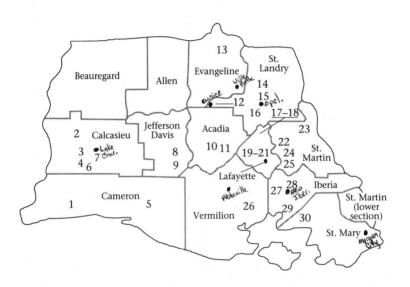

1. Sabine National Wildlife Refuge
2. DeQuincy Railroad Museum
3. Brimstone Museum
4. Creole Nature Trail
5. Little Pecan Island
6. Imperial Calcasieu Museum
7. Charpentier Historic District
8. Jennings
9. Lake Arthur Park
10. Belizaire's Cajun Restaurant
11. Rayne
12. The Liberty Center for the Performing Arts
13. Louisiana State Arboretum
14. Steamboat Warehouse
15. Opelousas Museum and Interpretive Center
16. Chrétien Point Plantation
17. La Maison de Campagne
18. Prudhomme's Cajun Cafe
19. Vermilionville
20. Cypress Lake
21. Acadian Village
22. Mulate's Cajun Restaurant
23. Pat's Fisherman's Wharf Restaurant
24. Longfellow-Evangeline State Commemorative Area
25. St. Martin de Tours Church Square
26. Abbeville
27. Live Oak Gardens
28. Shadows-on-the-Teche
29. Avery Island
30. Oaklawn Manor

Southwest Louisiana

Cameron Parish

Forming the heel of the Louisiana boot, the parishes of Cameron, Calcasieu (KAL-ka-shoe), Beauregard, Allen, and Jefferson Davis compose what was once called Imperial Calcasieu.

Made up mostly of marshlands and bayous, Cameron is Louisiana's largest parish. If you enter the state's southwestern corner via Interstate 10, consider either making a side trip to the ◆ **Sabine National Wildlife Refuge,** a major stop on the **Creole Nature Trail,** or taking the entire 105-mile driving tour. Because the trail starts and ends in Calcasieu Parish, a description of the route is included under that heading. The section on Little Pecan Island in Cameron Parish follows the Rockefeller Wildlife Refuge portion.

In either case take the Sulphur exit off Interstate 10 and turn south on State Route 27 (which is also the Creole Nature Trail). To reach the Sabine Refuge headquarters, proceed about 25 miles.

At the visitors' center you'll find an interpretive area, media room, wildlife exhibits, and information on the area's ecology. Displays demonstrate the importance of marshlands and the role the refuge plays in waterfowl and wildlife management.

An animated exhibit features the realistic figure of a Cajun fisherman sitting on a wharf, surrounded by marsh birds with attendant alligator. A close look reveals a snake under the wharf and a flounder in the water. At the press of a button, the fisherman launches into a tale, in Cajun dialect, about the area's history. He stands up, speaks of the value of the marshlands, and then reseats himself.

For a close-up view of the marshlands, you can take a self-guided tour along a nature trail, 4 miles south of the headquarters building. The 1.5-mile footpath changes from concrete to wooden walkway when it crosses the trail's water portions. For this hike bring along your binoculars and insect repellent. As you follow the footpath, you're likely to see alligators, especially on warm days when they surface to sun themselves. While these creatures may look lazy and sluggish, they can hurtle into fast-forward in a heartbeat, so it behooves one to maintain a respectful distance at all times. In cooler weather you'll spot small furry animals such as nutria, rabbits, and raccoons. Red wolves, foxes, and deer live here, too.

Bird-watchers will be beside themselves with glee. This refuge has a national reputation for being one of the country's best birding areas. Some 300 species of fowl consider the refuge either home or a nice place for a holiday. Established in 1937 mainly as a wintering area for migratory geese and ducks, the refuge also serves as home to the peregrine falcon.

About midway along the trail, you can climb a flight of wooden steps to an observation tower for a better view of this area of wetlands just above the Gulf of Mexico.

Popular times to visit are from mid-April to mid-May, when spring birds migrate, and September, when fall migration starts. The prime time for observing the refuge's waterfowl is from mid-November through January. Bird-watching, hiking, and nature study are year-round activities, but fishing is allowed only from March 1 through October 15.

You may use the marshlands trail from one hour before sunrise until one hour after sunset. The visitors' center is open from 7:00 A.M. to 4:00 P.M. Monday through Friday and from noon until 4:00 P.M. on Saturdays, Sundays, and holidays. Call (318) 762-3816 for additional information. There's no admission charge.

CALCASIEU PARISH

Railroad buffs might like to start exploring the state's southwestern portion at DeQuincy, reached by taking Route 27 north. Once a rowdy frontier town with eight saloons to serve a transient population of some 200 persons, DeQuincy managed to live down its early reputation after the railroad's arrival when it began attracting more serious settlers.

Both the ◆ **DeQuincy Railroad Museum** and the DeQuincy Chamber of Commerce occupy the Kansas City Southern Railroad's original depot at 218 Lake Charles Avenue. Musuem exhibits include a 1913 steam locomotive, coal car, vintage caboose, and several restored rail cars. You'll also see telegraph and railroad equipment, local historical memorabilia such as tickets and timetables dating from the early 1900s, uniforms, and an old mail pouch. You may admire the ticket agent's ability to concentrate as he sits before an antique typewriter absorbed by his work and apparently oblivious to all activity around him . . . until you realize that he's a mannequin.

Except for Wednesday when the museum is open from 1:00 to 5:00 P.M., weekday hours are 8:00 A.M. to 5:00 P.M. and from 1:00 to 5:00 P.M. on Saturday and Sunday. Call (318) 786–2823 for more information.

After leaving DeQuincy take Route 27 south to Sulphur and turn right on U.S. Highway 90 to reach Picard Road. The ◆ **Brimstone Museum,** located at 800 Picard Road, is housed in a railroad depot, and a one-ton block of sulphur marks the spot. You'll see a wildlife diorama, an antique medical instrument collection, photos of the town during its sulphur-mining heyday, and other exhibits related to the southwestern region.

The museum's focus concerns the history of the American sulphur industry, which started here, thanks to the ingenuity of Herman Frasch. Although it was no secret that sulphur deposits existed in the area, nobody knew how to tap this wealth. Extracting the yellow mineral from its underground home remained in the realm of the impossible until scientist/inventor Frasch solved the problem. He came up with a superheating water process that led to the commercial production of sulphur in this country. (Prior to 1900 almost all sulphur came from Sicily.) The Brimstone Museum, established in 1976, commemorates Frasch's contribution. A display and short movie describe both the Frasch process and sulphur's importance to modern society. Among other things sulphur is used in making medicines, rayon, fertilizers, insecticides, paper pulp, matches, and gunpowder.

The museum is open Monday through Friday from 9:30 A.M. to 5:00 P.M. Call (318) 527–7142. Admission is free.

From Sulphur you can either drive directly into the city of Lake Charles or take the long way around via the ◆ **Creole Nature Trail.** If you opt for the trail, be sure to pick up a self-guided tour brochure before leaving the Brimstone Museum. The Creole Nature Trail, which winds through the southern part of Calcasieu Parish and most of Cameron Parish, provides a good introduction to the area, but you need to allow at least half a day to complete the circuit—longer if you're prone to dally.

Few parts of the country look the same as they did when early settlers arrived. This is one of the few. At places along the way, one must mentally subtract civilized man's clutter, but even so, the land looks much as it did in earlier days. To some people this area might appear desolate, but the more discerning will recognize a singular environment teeming with life.

Starting in Sulphur, the Creole Nature Trail follows Route 27 down to the Gulf of Mexico, heads east along the coast, and backtracks before going north to Lake Charles. Marked by signs with an alligator logo, the trail follows state highways, which change during the route.

Along the way you'll pass through Hackberry, the crab capital of the world. Because hard-shell blue crabs are so plentiful here, you might be inclined to try your luck at crabbing. The basic equipment boils down to two pieces: a net to scoop up the crabs and a bucket to hold them. You can buy crabbing supplies at one of the area bait shops. With net in hand you can walk along a pier and capture any crabs you see on pilings, or you can wade in shallow water and scoop them up before they scurry away. Then there's the string-and-bait method. This entails attaching a one-ounce fishing weight plus a chunk of meat or fish to a string about 20 feet long. Toss the loaded line into the water, preferably near rocks or a dock. When you feel a slight tug, slowly pull the string toward you, keeping the net submerged and as still as possible so that it will look like part of the underwater scenery. As long as it's in the water, the crab will cling to the line. When it gets close enough, sweep it into your net. You have to be swift and synchronized, or the crab will win. After you collect enough crabs to constitute a meal, you can trade your bucket for a cookbook.

Just past Hackberry the driving tour intersects the Sabine Wildlife Refuge (described under Cameron Parish). Continue south on Route 27 toward Holly Beach (also called the Cajun Riviera) on the Gulf of Mexico. If you're a birder, you might want to get off the trail here and travel west on Route 82. This takes you to Johnson's Bayou and the Holleyman Bird Sanctuary, a popular bed and breakfast stop for many migrating songbirds crossing the Gulf each spring and fall.

From Holly Beach, the Creole Nature Trail stretches eastward along State Routes 27 and 82. Just before reaching Cameron, you'll drive aboard a fifty-car ferry that transports you across the Calcasieu Ship Channel. For eastward-bound travelers the trip is free, but those heading west pay a toll of $1.00 per car. If you step to the rail, you might catch a special performance by porpoises, who frequently put on a free show for ferry passengers. Back on the road in Cameron, you'll pass shrimp boats moored only a few yards from the highway. After Cameron your coastal trek takes you to Creole, Oak Grove, and Grand Chenier (shuh-NEAR). Along the way you'll see stranded sand and shell ridges, called "cheniers," from which groves of live oaks grow despite constant contact with salt water.

To shorten the drive you can skip Grand Chenier and take Route 27 north at Oak Grove. You'll pass by rice fields and pastures of cows—some nonchalantly grazing as cattle egrets perch on their backs.

Continue east on Route 82 if you want to visit the **Rockefeller Wildlife Refuge**. The refuge is open for sightseeing and fishing from March 1 through December 1. At the visitors' center, you'll see a display of artifacts from *El Nuevo Constant,* an eighteenth-century Spanish merchant vessel that sank off the Cameron coast. You may spot some alligators if you go exploring. The refuge has an international reputation as a major alligator research center. For more information, call (318) 538–2165 or (318) 538–2276.

After you leave the refuge, you'll have to do some backtracking. You can follow your trail map or choose another option. Routes 384, 385, and 14 (or variations thereof) all lead to Lake Charles. In any case, you'll be approaching the area's largest city from its southern side.

If you want to get away from it all, head north to ◆ **Little Pecan Island**, a place so remote it's not on your map. A visit to Little Pecan, located roughly midway between Rockefeller and Lacassine National Wildlife Refuge, requires making advance arrangements with The Nature Conservancy. Great for birding and fishing, the island lies about 10 miles inland from the Gulf of Mexico and stands only 5 feet above sea level. "Little Pecan is the oldest and highest chenier on the North American continent," says preserve manager Raphael Richard.

Arriving at the island represents an adventure in itself. Fortunately, you can leave the navigating to Raphael, who will meet you at Gaspar Landing and transport you on an 8-mile boat trip along the Mermentau River. As for locating the landing, you'll get a map from The Nature Conservancy, and you also can request directions at Rockefeller.

At the island, you'll see a lodge, a string of outbuildings, and massive oak trees trailing streamers of Spanish moss. A live oak forest occupies the chenier's west end, and cypress trees (including one 400-year-old survivor) stud the marshland. You will catch glimpses of alligators, shorebirds, deer, and other wildlife.

A former hunting lodge offers rustic but comfortable accommodations—seven bedrooms with twin beds, four dorm-type bathrooms, a sauna, great room with fireplace, recreation room, and dining room. A nearby cabin sleeps six persons. The facility runs $75 per adult and $37.50 per child (under twelve) per night with a six-person minimum. This price includes boat transportation to and from the lodge and a guided tour of the preserve. For an additional fee, food will be provided, or you can bring your own. If you're lucky, you can feast on fresh crab, cooked on the premises. (When I visited, someone had just landed and iced down a thirty-pound catfish.) Although the island may be visited year-round, the best months to go are from March through May (when you might see an ocean of wild iris in bloom) or during October and November. Don't forget mosquito repellent. For reservations or more information on this, one of the last remaining pristine cheniers, write to Louisiana Nature Conservancy, P.O. Box 4125, Baton Rouge, LA 70821 or call (504) 338–1040.

After your island excursion, head northwest to Lake Charles. When you arrive at this inland location, you may think that the sandy beach studded with palm trees on the shore of Lake Charles is a mirage. But man-made North Beach is indeed real—and the only inland white sand beach on the entire Gulf Coast. A drive over the Jean Lafitte Bridge affords a panoramic view of the beach, which borders Interstate 10.

This area was once **Jean Lafitte's** stomping ground. The "Gentleman Pirate" was a poetic sort who allegedly stashed some of his treasure in nearby watery mazes. To this day Lake Charles still plays host to pirates. Just visit in the spring when the city celebrates Contraband Days, starting with "Lafitte's invasion." The pirate's swashbuckling arrival sets off a jolly two-week round of parades, parties, pageants, boat races, and other festivities. In true buccaneering tradition one event features local officials "walking the plank."

Lafitte's loot may be hopelessly hidden, but you'll discover treasure aplenty at the **Cottage Shops,** clustered around Hodges, Alamo, and Common streets. Some dozen downtown specialty shops offer items ranging from antique armoires and handmade quilts to Cajun upside-down pickles and stained glass.

At 2620 Hodges Street you'll find Nana's Cupboard, brimming over with unique gift items, linens, collector dolls, pottery, and quilts. Nana's Cupboard is open Monday through Saturday from 9:30 A.M. until 5:30 P.M.

If you're a coffee lover, don't pass up **The Louisiana Market** at 2710 Hodges Street. Owner-manager Bill McCain daily brews up a different flavor from his line of specialty coffees. You'll enjoy sipping coffee as you browse through aisles of authentic Cajun/Creole specialty foods and gifts. From hand-carved ducks to hot pepper jelly, a gift list can be taken care of here in one fell swoop. Shelves are loaded with seasonings, condiments, pickles, hurricane mixes (for drinks, not disasters), recipe books, iron skillets, chef's aprons—everything to make a gourmet happy. Saturday visitors can expect a tantalizing sample of a regional specialty such as jambalaya or red beans and rice. Market hours are Monday through Saturday from 10:00 A.M. until 5:30 P.M.

Don't miss Somewhere In Time at 2802 Hodges Street. Here you'll encounter all sorts of delightful things to see and smell. The shop stocks Victorian, traditional, and country items including laces, linens, wreaths, soaps, potpourri, English teapots, antiques, and more. Hours are Monday through Saturday from 9:30 A.M. until 5:30 P.M. Pick up a pamphlet and continue your treasure hunt through the other Cottage Shops, all located nearby.

To acquaint yourself with the history of Lake Charles, you can visit the ◆ **Imperial Calcasieu Museum,** located on the corner of Ethel and Sallier streets. The museum stands on the site of a cabin built by early settler Charles Sallier (sal-YAY), for whom the city was named.

Look left as you enter, and you'll see the steering wheel from the paddle wheeler *Borealis Rex*. In earlier days this ship served as the only link between Lake Charles and Cameron, located on Calcasieu Lake's southern side. Each Wednesday a crowd gathered to welcome the steamer bringing mail, freight, and passengers.

Along the museum's right aisle, you'll pass a furnished parlor, kitchen, and bedroom, all depicting scenes from yesteryear.

Unusual antiques include a square grand piano made in Baltimore, and a massive Prudent Mallard bed of rosewood. There are household items—antique china and cooking utensils, hand-pieced quilts, period clothing, a toy collection, and even a wreath made of human hair.

A collection of personalized shaving mugs adds to the decor in the museum's Gay Nineties barbershop, and a recreated country store nearby features nostalgic merchandise. A pharmacist stands ready to dispense remedies in his apothecary, an original section from a downtown drugstore. You'll see a physician's travel kit and a glass-cased display of bottles in a rainbow of colors. Be sure to notice the ornate set of ironstone apothecary jars made in France during the early sixteenth century.

A Civil War flag from the Battle of Mobile Bay is on display in the War Room. You'll also see a uniform worn by General Claire Chennault, who led the famed Flying Tigers. This exhibit includes Mrs. Chennault's wedding gown and going-away costume, books, and various items of historical significance.

A Geneva Bible, an Edison phonograph, and a stereopticon are all treasures you won't want to overlook. The museum features a fine collection of bird and animal prints by John James Audubon as well as excerpts from the diary he kept while working in Louisiana. There's an exhibit of Lafitte memorabilia with a copy of the pirate's journal, published over a century after his death. (Maybe it contains a clue as to where he concealed his contraband.) Admission fee is modest.

Don't leave without stepping out to the museum's backyard for a view of the venerable **Sallier Oak.** Some tree experts estimate this magnificent live oak to be about 300 years old. Whether or not the tree has weathered three centuries, it carries its age well, and its credentials include membership in the Live Oak Society. With branches dipping almost to the ground, this inviting oak would fulfill any child's tree-climbing fantasies.

A survivor, the Sallier Oak has endured its share of adversity. You can still see the heavy chains used to bind the tree when a 1918 hurricane split the trunk. A storm wreaked havoc on its west side in 1930, and lightning struck the oak in 1938, severely damaging its southwest side. But the tree still stands tall—56 feet—and projects an air of serenity. Its limbs, adorned with resurrection fern, extend about 125 feet. (Switch to your wide-angle lens if you hope to get a picture.)

Although the Sallier Oak may be visited at any time, the museum's hours are Tuesday through Friday from 10:00 A.M. to 5:00 P.M. and on Saturday and Sunday from to 1:00 to 5:00 P.M. The museum's number is (318) 439–3797.

A walking or driving tour of the city's historic ✦ **Charpentier Historic District** takes you through some twenty square blocks of homes dating from the Victorian era. Because many of the houses in this area were constructed before professional architects arrived on the scene, they express the individuality of their various builders. Area carpenters created their own patterns by changing rooflines, porch placements, and other exterior features. Sometimes they combined traditional design elements in new ways. A typical house constructed of native cypress and longleaf yellow pine might feature an odd number of columns with a bay on one side and a porch on the other. This distinctive look now commands an architectural category all its own—Lake Charles Style.

The Southwest Louisiana Convention and Visitors Bureau produces an illustrated brochure that outlines a walking-driving route through the historic district. You can request one by calling 1–800–456–SWLA or (318) 436–9588.

If you have offspring in tow, consider stopping by **The Children's Museum** while in this area. It's located at 925 Enterprise Boulevard. Youngsters can indulge their curiosity and creative instincts through various participatory programs. They can don uniforms and pretend to fight fires, or broadcast their own news from a television-studio setting.

Changing exhibits explore areas of natural and physical science, history, art, crafts, and geography. (When I asked the floor monitor to suggest an upper age limit for children who might enjoy the museum's offerings, she replied that some of their participants qualify for Social Security.)

Public hours are Tuesday through Friday from 2:00 to 5:00 P.M., Saturday from 10:00 A.M. to 4:00 P.M., and Sunday from 2:00 to 5:00 P.M. During the summer the museum is closed on Wednesdays as well as the last week of August through the first two weeks of September. Call (318) 433–9421 or (318) 433–9420. Admission is modest. Adults, if accompanied by a child, are admitted at no charge.

During your Lake Charles visit, you may want to check with **McNeese State University,** which offers special concerts and exhibits throughout the year. To find out what might be on tap, call the college at (318) 477–2520.

Traveling east from Lake Charles, most drivers take Interstate 10. Route 14, however, runs south of the interstate (more in a meandering fashion than parallel) and offers some scenic vistas denied travelers on the interstate (albeit periodic road signs caution motorists about speeding on a substandard highway). If you do opt for Route 14, keep in mind that it takes longer, but you might see such striking vistas as entire fields white with egrets. Also you won't get "arrested" for not stopping in Jennings, as you might if you take the interstate. It's true—passing up Jennings constitutes a crime—if you get caught, that is. To learn more, read on.

JEFFERSON DAVIS PARISH

Persons driving through this part of the state on Interstate 10 risk possible arrest if they fail to take the ◆**Jennings** exit. Typical case: Mr. L., his wife, and two children were traveling along said route when stopped by the local sheriff. Mr. L. was neither speeding nor breaking any laws. His crime? Not stopping in Jennings. Each year the local Optimist Club "arrests" an out-of-state driver for not stopping in Jennings. The party is charged, tried, and sentenced. Any plea-bargaining attempts by a court-appointed attorney are thrown out by presiding judges. The guilty party is sentenced to eat lunch with the Optimist Club and drive off with a load of gifts (plus a tank of gas) from area merchants. Also, he or she must promise to stop in Jennings if passing that way again.

Some travelers bypass highways entirely and simply fly in. An airport, adjacent to the interstate, attracts all sorts of "fly people"—from Cessna owners to Stearman pilots—who migrate to Jennings the third weekend in October for the annual end-of-the-season fly-in. Pilots practice formation flying in pairs and in groups because the airport allows "free flight" if sessions are performed by seasoned veterans. Pilots can taxi right up to the door of the local Holiday Inn. (From cockpit to motel room might mean a hop, skip, and jump of some 50 yards.)

75

Whether your visit in Jennings results from coercion or choice, all sorts of delights await you off the beaten path. Start with the **Louisiana Oil and Gas Park,** just north of town (and visible from Interstate 10). Louisiana's first oil well produced "black gold" on September 21, 1901, just 5 miles northeast of town in a rice field that belonged to farmer Jules Clement. The park, which commemorates that significant event, contains a replica of the small wooden oil rig used to drill the first well. Next to the derrick stands an early **Acadian-style house** where the Visitor Information Center is located.

An ideal place to take a driving break, the public recreation area includes a jogging trail, picnic facilities, playground equipment, a lake, and flocks of ducks and geese that act as a welcoming committee. You also can see **Château des Cocodries** (a live alligator exhibit).

Replica of an Acadian House

The lake is a great place to wet a fishing line and try for blue gill or largemouth bass. (State law requires a fishing license.)

Select a table and spread a picnic, but save some sandwich crusts for the ducks—they consider it their duty to dispose of any leftovers. Maybe the ducks should be thanked for the trophy designating Jennings as Louisiana's cleanest city. After winning the "Cleanest City" award three years in a row, Jennings received the trophy for its permanent collection.

Jennings celebrated its first century in 1988. The town was named for a railroad contractor, Jennings McComb. When the railroad came through this section in 1880, McComb erected most of the depots, so railroad officials honored him by giving his first name to the unpopulated area around one of the depots. (A town in Mississippi had already claimed his last name.) Sure enough, the blank spot on the prairie began to attract settlers, mostly from the Midwest. Farmers did not have to first clear the land of trees—there were none. Homesteaders received extra land for planting trees on their property. They also planted crops they had raised in their home states of Iowa, Illinois, Indiana, and Missouri, and began to experiment with rice-farming techniques. By 1894 more than a thousand acres of rice grew on the Cajun prairie surrounding Jennings.

Later a number of Yankees who had fought in the area during the Civil War returned afterward to settle here. The local cemetery contains quite a few more graves for the Blue than the Gray. Consequently Jennings came to be known as a "northern town on Southern soil."

Don't leave Jennings without visiting the **Zigler Museum**, acclaimed for its outstanding fine arts collection. To get there from the park, take Route 26 south (going under the interstate) until you reach Clara Street where you'll turn left. At 411 Clara Street, you'll see the museum, a white-columned structure with colonial styling. Two gallery wings were added to the former home of Ruth and Fred Zigler to create this facility.

The central gallery, with paintings and sculpture by both state and national artists, presents a new exhibit each month. Nearby you'll see an antique handgun collection with more than fifty firearms ranging from Colts and dueling pistols to different types of derringers.

Realistic dioramas depicting the state's southwestern wildlife fill the east wing. The museum features a facsimile of John James Audubon's *Birds of America,* an edition that was duplicated from original plates in the National Audubon Society Folio. Don't overlook the wonderful wildfowl wood carvings.

The west wing houses the museum's permanent collection of works by both European and American artists such as Rembrandt and Whistler. From the Middle Ages to the present, the paintings take you on a journey through art history.

The Zigler's Louisiana Gallery often displays the work of such state artists such as Clementine Hunter, William Tolliver, and George Rodrigue (rod-REEG). A Cajun painter, Rodrigue regularly wins international awards for his oils. His *Aioli Dinner* and other paintings feature people (almost always dressed in white) portrayed against dark backgrounds. All project a haunting quality. You can see more of the artist's work at the Rodrigue Gallery in Lafayette and New Orleans.

Closed on Mondays and holidays, the Zigler Museum is open Tuesday through Saturday from 9:00 A.M. to 5:00 P.M. and on Sunday from 1:00 to 5:00 P.M. Admission is modest. The museum's number is (318) 824–0114.

Continue to the end of Clara Street, which runs into Cary Avenue. Next, turn on Second Street and go to State Street. At 710 North State Street stands **Our Lady Help of Christians Catholic Church,** one of the town's historic buildings. Step inside the sanctuary for a view of the windows in glowing stained glass, made in Germany. In designing the church, Father Joseph Peeters, a native of Belgium, was inspired by Notre Dame in Paris. You'll recognize some of the great Gothic cathedral's characteristics, such as the three arched entrances, in this smaller, plainer version. Constructed of homemade concrete blocks that were cast on the building site, the church was dedicated in 1916 after a building period of several years.

A short walk takes you to the Marian Prayer Park, located adjacent to the church on the rectory's south side. From here you'll do a bit of backtracking. While retracing your drive, you might want to take a ride along Cary Avenue for a look at the lovely old homes. Architectural features, reflecting a midwestern influence, include turrets, balconies, porches, and gables accented with gingerbread woodwork and fish-scale shingles.

Take a sentimental journey to the **W. H. Tupper General Merchandise Museum** at 311 North Main Street. The museum's stock came from a store built near Elton in 1910 by Mary and W. H. Tupper for their farm workers. Although the store closed in 1949, the contents remained intact—frozen in time for four decades. The store's original inventory consisted of toys, cosmetics, dishes, drugs, cooking utensils, seeds, fans, jewelry, bluejean overalls, and other items that bring back memories. Adding to the authenticity, staff members wear vintage clothing.

You'll also see a large selection of baskets made by members of the Chitimacha and Coushatta tribes. The Coushattas live 3 miles northwest of Elton on the northern edge of the parish. Museum hours are Tuesday through Saturday from 10:00 A.M. to 6:00 P.M. Admission is modest. Call (318) 821–5532.

Take time to browse through the **Old Magnolia Gift Shoppe,** also housed here. You'll find great gifts and souvenirs such as Cajun cookbooks, Louisiana products, jellies, children's books, toys, crafts, paintings, and antiques. In a nearby room called The Back Porch, you can watch members of the Cajun Country Quilting Guild at work and see a selection of their handiwork.

Also sharing the Tupper building, the **Telephone Pioneer Museum of Lousiana** features displays of phones from past to present with exhibits going back to switchboards and party lines.

Afterward, stop by **Boudin King**, located at 906 West Division Street in a residential district. No trip to Cajun country would be complete without sampling boudin (boo-dan). The state legislature passed an act declaring Jennings the Boudin Capital of the Universe, and you would be hard-pressed to find a better place for trying this specialty. Restaurant owner Ellis Cormier, whose customers call him the Boudin King, defines his boudin as a mixture of pork, spices, and long-grain rice. Louisiana French people have been partial to boudin for more than two centuries, and Cormier follows an Acadian recipe that's been passed down in his family for generations. To prime pork he adds parsley, peppers, green onions, and rice (cooked separately). The resulting mixture is stuffed into a sausage casing, then steamed and served warm.

A great appetizer, boudin comes in links, both mild and hot. If you can't decide which to try, Cormier will let you sample each, but he suggests starting with mild and working your way up to hot (my favorite).

When June and Ellis Cormier turned their neighborhood grocery store into a restaurant featuring boudin, local folks predicted a short run for the establishment because the Cormiers decided not to serve alcohol. Customers joked that it took both "a pound of boudin and a six-pack of beer to make a seven-course Cajun dinner." That was in 1974, and if you stop by the Boudin King today, you'll probably have to stand in line.

Although boudin gets star billing here, the menu offers other items such as chicken-and-sausage gumbo, fried crawfish, catfish, chicken, and red beans and rice with smoked sausage. You also can buy hogshead cheese, a sort of pâté especially good when spread on crackers.

Prices are economical. Boudin King, which closes on Sundays, operates from 8:00 A.M. until 9:00 P.M. Monday through Saturday. Call (318) 824–6593.

Before leaving Jefferson Davis Parish, take Route 26 down to Lake Arthur, 9 miles south of Jennings. For some picturesque scenery drive along the edge of the lake, lined with lovely old homes. Cypress trees, with swaying Spanish moss trailing from their branches, stand knee-deep in Lake Arthur. In this laid-back resort area, you can fish, hunt, or watch the cranes, egrets, herons, and other birds.

◆**Lake Arthur Park** offers a bandstand, pavilions, picnic facilities, and an enclosed swimming area with lifeguards on duty. Throughout the year the town stages events at the park. Spring brings a Sailboat Regatta with a weekend of entertainment including boat races and a dance on Main Street. Booths feature food, drinks, and displays of arts and crafts. The park is also the setting for a star-spangled Fourth of July Celebration, a Labor Day Seafood Festival, and a Christmas Festival with thousands of lights. For more information on Lake Arthur events, call the Town Hall at (318) 774–2211.

If hunger pangs hit while you're in Lake Arthur, head for **Nott's Corner**, located at 639 Arthur Avenue. But don't strain your eyes looking for street numbers—it's easier to watch for the giant crawfish outside the restaurant.

Owners Irene and Gummy Hanks dish up good Cajun food in a dining room decorated with original photographs of local historical hotels and homes. Depending on the season, they serve boiled crawfish six days a week. When you find yourself facing a platter piled with the steaming red crustaceans, don't be shy about requesting assistance on matters of procedure. Nearby connoisseurs will gladly instruct you in the art of peeling crawfish, also known as crawdads, or mudbugs. You may prefer to remain a rank amateur—which is not without its advantages. For instance, if you have trouble getting the hang of crawfish peeling, someone may just decide it's easier to do it *for* you than to teach you how. Then all that's left to do is dip the peeled portion into some scrumptious sauce. Keep in mind that while the tidbit is tasty, it's also hot, so you'll require lots of something cold to drink.

In addition to boiled crawfish, Nott's Corner serves crawfish *étouffée* (ay-two-FAY), crawfish dinners, fried shrimp, oysters, catfish, frog legs, stuffed shrimp, stuffed crab, and steaks. Prices are moderate.

Open for breakfast through dinner, the restaurant serves from 7:00 A.M. to 9:00 P.M. Sunday and Tuesday through Thursday and from 7:00 A.M. to 10:00 P.M. on Friday and Saturday. It is closed on Monday. For more information, call (318) 774–2332.

After your delectable repast, drive back to Route 26 and travel north until the road intersects U.S. Highway 90. You'll then go east, passing by acres of rice fields on your way to Crowley, the Rice Center of America.

ACADIA PARISH

Each October Crowley hosts the International Rice Festival with rice-eating contests, fiddling and accordion competitions, parades, a street fair, a livestock show, and other events.

The **Rice Museum**, located on U.S. Highway 90 west in Crowley, features exhibits on Acadian culture, local history, and the rice industry. You'll see a working miniature rice mill, antique farm equipment, and tools. Exhibits explain the planting, cultivating, and harvesting of rice as well as its importance to Cajun culture. There are also displays of different products and by-products in which rice is used.

The museum, staffed by volunteers, is open by appointment only. For more information contact the Crowley Chamber of Commerce at (318) 788–0177.

For a good meal in Crowley, head to ✦**Belizaire's Cajun Restaurant,** located at 2307 North Parkerson. Featured dishes include fried alligator, blackened fish, crawfish, and seafood gumbo, but you'll find plenty of other items such as the two-step special, a combination of stuffed catfish and crawfish with pasta in a creamy cheese sauce. Children under six are served without charge.

You can dine while you absorb some regional culture by watching video productions on Cajun festivals, alligator hunting, and antebellum homes. Afterward you can dance away the calories doing the Cajun two-step to live music (from 8:00 P.M. until closing on Thursday, Friday, and Saturday and also from 4:00 to 8:00 P.M. on Sunday). The restaurant, which also offers souvenirs and gifts, opens daily at 11:00 A.M. and serves until 10:00 P.M. Saturday hours are from 5:00 to 11:00 P.M. On Sunday the restaurant opens at 11:00 A.M. and closes at 8:00 P.M. Reservations are recommended. Call (318) 788–2501.

On your way out of Crowley, go by the courthouse square. Starting on Main Street you can drive through the downtown historic district, which features some eight blocks of lovely Victorian homes. From here take U.S. Highway 90 east to reach Rayne, about 7 miles from Crowley and 13 miles west of Lafayette.

If you didn't realize that ◆**Rayne** is the Frog Capital of the World, you will before you depart. The first clue might be big colorful murals on the sides of old buildings—all depicting frogs in one fashion or another. On your driving tour be sure to notice the interesting aboveground cemetery.

Mark Twain's jumping frog of Calaveras County would have been in his element here, happy among his peers. This town is filled not only with bona fide frogs, but with pictures of frogs, statues of frogs, literature about frogs, and even frog factories. What do frog factories export? Frog legs for restaurant menus and specimens for scientific purposes, of course. Besides being the center of Louisiana's frog industry, Rayne also ranks as one of the world's largest shippers of frogs.

For fifty-one weeks of the year, Rayne could be considered off the beaten path. During the third week in September, however, the world beats a path to its door—during a fun-filled Frog Festival, which features fireworks, frog-cooking contests, frog derbies, and frog beauty contests. On the first and third weekends each month, you can visit Rayne's Antique Mall in the old Mervine Kahn Building at 113 Louisiana Avenue; hours are 9:00 A.M. to 5:00 P.M.

After leaving Rayne, return to Crowley and take State Route 13 north to Eunice.

ST. LANDRY PARISH

Consider a short trip on the Acadiana Trail (also U.S. Highway 190), which runs through a number of interesting towns such as Eunice, the state's crawfish-processing center. Depending on the season you'll see acres of rice growing or thousands of crawfish traps in this area where fields do double duty. Now a major agricultural industry, crawfish farming utilizes flooded rice fields during winter and early spring.

Complement your trip to Cajun country by taking in a performance at ◆ **The Liberty Center for the Performing Arts** on the corner of South Second Street and Park Avenue in downtown Eunice. Every Saturday night from 6:00 to 8:00 P.M., *Rendezvous des Cajuns,* a live radio show, features a lineup of musicians and entertainers such as Cajun humorist A. J. Smith from Lake Charles. Don't miss the outstanding exhibits at neighboring **Acadian Cultural Center of Jean Lafitte Historical Park & Preserve.**

About a block away, **Nick's on 2nd** serves a variety of favorites from po-boys, shrimp salad, and stuffed flounder to lamb chops and eggplant pirogue. Formerly a men's bar, the restaurant at 123 South Second Street has been been remodeled in a pink, green, and black color scheme. Call (318) 457-4921.

While in Eunice, stop by **Walnut Street Society** and browse through the shop's displays of decorating accessories, flowers, and gifts. Located at 151 West Walnut, the store is owned by Myrna and Garrett Miller. Call (318) 457-1471.

Overnight visitors can make reservations at **The Seale Guesthouse,** located 2 miles south of Eunice on State Route 13. The country house with wraparound porch offers lodging options such as rooms with private baths, suites with shared baths, or a two-bedroom guest cottage. Owners Jennifer and Mark Seale collected antiques and nostalgic items to furnish the house. Rates are standard to moderate. For more information call (318) 457-3753.

Each fall, Eunice hosts the Louisiana Folklife Festival—a feast for the senses where you can hear Cajun, zydeco, blues, and jazz music; smell and taste tempting specialties such as boudin, gumbo, and jambalaya; and watch artisans make crafts in the tradition of their ancestors. For more information on the festival or other events, call the Eunice Chamber of Commerce at (318) 457–2565.

After visiting Eunice, head north to Ville Platte.

EVANGELINE PARISH

While passing through Ville Platte, plan to stop by **Floyd's Record Shop** on Highway 167 south where you'll find not only film, photographic supplies, and regional books but a comprehensive inventory of traditional Cajun music with recordings by artists dating to the 1930s. If Floyd Soileau (pronounced swallow) is available, he can give you the history of the sounds he helped preserve by recording these musicians. The retail business is open six days a week. Call (318) 363–2138.

For dining, try **The Jungle Club** on Highway 167 west (Main Street), famous for its boiled crawfish trays (in season). This specialty comes in mild, hot, super hot, and extra super hot choices. Although the crawfish selections including *étouffée* and bisque remain favorites, the restaurant offers other outstanding dishes such as its award-winning gumbo. "We won a gold medal at the Heritage Festival for our red snapper *au gratin*," says Wendell Manuel, who owns the restaurant along with his uncle, Jesse Manuel. The Jungle Club opens daily at 5:30 P.M. and closes at 11:00 P.M. on Sunday through Thursday and at midnight on Friday and Saturday. Prices are moderate. Call (318) 363–9103.

About 6 miles north of Ville Platte, you'll find **Chicot State Park** on State Route 3042. With 6,500 acres of rolling hills and a 2,000-acre lake, the park offers plenty of recreation opportunities. Just beyond, you can visit ◆ **Louisiana State Arboretum** with inviting nature trails and footbridges interspersed among labeled specimens of native plants. Rambling through the forest and across hills, ravines, and creeks, you'll see birds, deer, and local flora such as pine, oak, magnolia, beech, dogwood, and papaws. "Over eighty different species of trees and over a hundred species of vines and shrubs grow here," says horticulturist Tom Hebert, who gives guided tours at 10:00 A.M. and 2:00 P.M. on Saturday and Sunday. The arboretum is open daily from dawn to dusk, and admission is free. Call (318) 363–6289. After your botanical outing, head for neighboring St. Landry Parish.

ST. LANDRY PARISH

In a tin shed near his Grand Prairie home, Joe Soileau practices an uncommon craft—making cowhide chair seats. From cleaning and curing the hides to producing finishing products such as rockers, baby chairs, footstools, and tom-tom drums, Joe takes great satisfaction in continuing a family tradition. Joe, who also sells insurance, watched his father and grandfather make chair covers from cowhide. To observe the chair-covering process or place an order, call Joe at (318) 826–3295.

Afterward, continue to Washington, one of the state's oldest permanent settlements. Located on Bayou Courtableau, Washington once bustled as steamboat town, and you can glimpse a bit of local history at Jack Womack's ◆**Steamboat Warehouse** on Main Street and enjoy a good meal at the same time. The large brick warehouse, built between 1819 and 1823 and restored as a restaurant in 1976, specializes in steaks and seafood. After dipping into one of Jack's specialties such as Catfish Lizzy topped with crawfish *étouffée* and hollandaise sauce, take time to look at lading bills and other documents displayed here. An 1870 shipment, for instance, included candles, claret, coffee, tea, table salt, pickles, apples, and nails. Except for Christmas Day and New Year's Day, the restaurant is open Tuesday through Thursday from 5:00 to 10:00 P.M. and Sunday 11:00 A.M. to 1:00 P.M. Call (318) 826–7227.

Many of Washington's historic homes, plantations, and buildings were constructed between 1780 and 1835, and some are open for tours and/or bed and breakfast. For more information, contact the Washington Museum and Tourist Center at (318) 826–3627 or Town Hall at (318) 826–3626.

After exploring Washington, head south to Opelousas.

On U.S. Highway 190 east, you'll find the **Jim Bowie Museum,** next to the tourist information center. Exhibits focus on Bowie's career, but there are also displays on Acadian culture along with old documents, photographs, farm equipment, and firearms.

During his boyhood Bowie lived here in a home that his father built on what is now the museum lawn. After serving for a while in the Louisiana legislature, Bowie moved to Texas, where he fought and died at the Alamo. While legend credits him with the invention of the bowie knife, some historians contend that this is not a fact, although Bowie may have contributed to the knife's design. The Jim Bowie Museum is open daily from 8:00 A.M. until 4:00 P.M., and there's no admission charge. Call (318) 948–6263.

The ◆ **Opelousas Museum and Interpretive Center** at 329 North Main Street presents a fascinating overview of local culture back to prehistoric times. Resident/writer Carola Ann Andrepont describes the area as "a melting pot or cultural gumbo" because the settlers came from many ethnic backgrounds. Named for an Indian tribe who occupied the site earlier, Opelousas became a bayou trading post for French and Indian interchange in 1720. This fertile area also attracted the Spanish around the same time. Displays in the main exhibit room spotlight the people—their agriculture, home and family, business and professions, music and food.

Among other things, the town pays tribute to the sweet potato's cousin with an annual Yambilee Festival the last weekend in October. Spring and fall Folklife Festivals focus on the "olden days." A **Zydeco Festival** is staged in nearby Plaisance each September, and you'll see a presentation on zydeco (ZI-da-ko), which might be described as a musical merger of such sounds as rhythm and blues, jazz, rock and roll, gospel, and Cajun music. Opelousas, the birthplace of this unique style, was the home of "Zydeco King," the late Clifton Chenier. Also, before leaving the main room, be sure to notice the exhibits on the Orphan Train and the 1914 Dunbar kidnapping case.

Another section contains the Geraldine Smith Welch doll collection. You'll see more than 400 dolls, grouped in categories from antiques and miniatures to pop culture.

The center also houses the **Louisiana Video Collection Library,** a valuable resource for delving into state history, and a section on the Civil War when Opelousas served as the state's capital for a brief period. You can visit the center from Wednesday through Sunday between 9:00 A.M. and 5:00 P.M. Call (318) 948–2589.

Before leaving town, stop by the **Palace Cafe** at 167 West Landry Street (Highway 190 west). Try Pete's fried chicken salad, the Grecian salad, or house specialty—baked eggplant stuffed

86

with crab. Top off your meal with the restaurant's famous baklava, a Greek pastry made with pecan butter and honey. Prices are economical to moderate.

Afterward, head toward ◆ **Chrétien Point Plantation.** From Opelousas get on Interstate 49 south. Take the exit for Sunset/Grand Coteau and drive through Sunset. This puts you on Route 93 south. After 3.8 miles you'll see the Bristol/Bosco road. Turn right, go one block, then take another right. Go 1 mile and Chrétien Point Plantation will be on your left.

Built by Hypolite Chrétien II in 1831, this grand Greek Revival house features both a window and staircase that served as models for those in Tara during the filming of *Gone with the Wind*. The mansion stands on land that was a wedding gift from Chrétien's father, a rich cotton planter and close friend of Jean Lafitte, who frequently visited this plantation.

When Hypolite II died soon after moving into the mansion, his wife Félicité took over the reins and ran the large farming operation. On a mansion tour, your guide will tell you more stories about Félicité, a liberated woman who smoked cigars and played poker— supposedly her aptitude for gambling doubled the plantation's size to 10,000 acres. Local lore also holds that she shot a man (perhaps a pirate from Lafitte's crew) on the stairs when he broke in and refused to halt. Bloodstains, which partially show from beneath the carpet runner, remain on the steps.

Although the house survived the Civil War's ravage, the plantation's outbuildings were destroyed. Later, after the farm failed and dilapidation set in, the mansion served as a barn where animals roamed and hay was kept. Now restored to its former grandeur and furnished with nineteenth-century pieces and portraits, it is open for daily tours from 10:00 A.M. to 5:00 P.M. except for major holidays. The day's last tour starts at 4:00 P.M. Admission is moderate.

Visitors may also stay overnight here and enjoy a full plantation breakfast and use the pool and tennis courts. Bed-and-breakfast guests get a mansion tour and are welcomed with mint juleps on the gallery. Rates are moderate to deluxe. For reservations call (318) 233–7050 or (318) 662–5876.

As you drive through this part of the country, tune in to local radio stations, where you'll hear the unique sounds of Cajun

| dialect. Sometimes the news is broadcast in French
imes in English.
g to Interstate 49, you'll travel south toward Lafayette,
stopping first in Carencro.

LAFAYETTE PARISH

For a taste of Southern hospitality, make reservations at ◆ **La Maison de Campagne** (The Country House). Owners Joeann and Fred McLemore, who "fell in love with the B & B concept in Europe," will make you glad you came. You'll find this family-oriented bed and breakfast at 825 Kidder Road in Carencro, 7 miles north of Lafayette. Fronted by a lawn of trees featuring three massive oaks in a row, the large white house fits its setting perfectly, although it was originally built in Lafayette and moved here in sections. Special features include pecan floors and towering pocket parlor doors.

The McLemores furnished their home with antiques, crystal, and china collected throughout the world during Fred's army career. Be sure to notice the unusual old Bavarian box clock, golden oak pieces, and a walnut-covered poster bed in the Magnolia Room.

Breakfast actually starts with coffee brought to your room, which you might sip on the porch. The feast continues in the dining room with Joeann's "little fruity frappé," broiled grapefruit, oven omelet with tasso, buttermilk-banana-pecan pancakes with muscadine sauce, and homebaked bread. In season, guests may use the pool. Rates are moderate. For reservations call 1–800–368–7308 or (318) 896–6529.

Located at 4676 Northeast Evangeline Thruway off Interstate 49 about five minutes from the McLemores' home, ◆ **Prudhomme's Cajun Cafe** occupies a house dating from the late 1800s. Photographs, certificates, and awards (won by Prudhomme family members for their culinary expertise) line vestibule walls. The name "Prudhomme" is practically synonymous with good cooking. The restaurant is run by Enola, sister of famed New Orleans chef Paul Prudhomme. It was Prudhomme who put the spotlight on blackened redfish and Cajun cuisine.

The restaurant's specialties include blackened fish and meats, soft-shelled crawfish in sherry sauce, and stuffed catfish covered in cream sauce and sprinkled with slivers of *tasso* (a spicy Cajun ham). Another popular item is eggplant pirogue, in which eggplant halves are hollowed out, heaped with crabmeat, crawfish, and shrimp and topped with a cheese sauce and more shrimp. Vegetables, potatoes, and homemade white bread and jalapeño cornbread accompany each entrée. Diet-conscious diners can choose from such entrées as shrimp in cream sauce on fettuccine or marinated grilled chicken breast with vegetables. Chef Enola offers a special menu of reduced-calorie selections she created. You might like to purchase a copy of *Enola Prudhomme's Low-Calorie Cajun Cooking* before leaving the restaurant.

The restaurant, staffed by Prudhomme family members, offers daily luncheon specials and is open Tuesday through Saturday from 11:00 A.M. to 10:00 P.M. Sunday hours are 11:00 A.M. to 2:30 P.M. Call (318) 896–7964.

Continue south to reach Lafayette, the hub city of Acadiana. The Acadiana area, which comprises nearly one-third of Louisiana's sixty-four parishes, was settled by French Acadians who were ousted from Nova Scotia and New Brunswick by the British in 1755. Forced to leave their homes and property, families were broken up and sent to various destinations. Many eventually made their way to South Louisiana, where Acadians came to be known as "Cajuns."

During the 1770s a large number of Acadians settled in Lafayette (then called Vermilionville because of the nearby bayou's reddish color). In 1884 the town was renamed to honor Lafayette, the French general of American Revolutionary War fame. Now ◆**Vermilionville** has been reincarnated as a twenty-three-acre living-history attraction focusing on Cajun/Creole culture. Located at 1600 Surrey Street across from the airport, the complex features entertainment, craft demonstrations, and an operating farm typical of those in the eighteenth century. Also, a cooking school staff demonstrates Creole and Cajun methods of food preparation.

Geese strut about, honking at visitors, and costumed storytellers, musicians, and craftspeople re-create the folklife of bayou settlers from 1765 to 1890. As Acadian descendants, many staffers switch easily from speaking English to Cajun French. A hand-pulled ferry takes you across *Petit Bayou* to Fausse Pointe where you'll meet Broussard family members such as Camille and Eliza.

89

The couple speak and behave as people did in the 1840s and may inquire about your strange apparatus called a camera, your attire, or some unfamiliar expression. Except for Christmas Day and New Year's Day, Vermilionville opens daily 9:00 A.M. to 5:00 P.M. There is an admission fee. Call 1–800–992–2968 or (318) 233–4077.

A good place to start a city tour is the **Lafayette Museum** at 1122 Lafayette Street. The home of Louisiana's first Democratic governor, Alexandre Mouton, this antebellum townhouse contains antiques, Civil War relics, and historic documents. Go upstairs and see the lavish hand-beaded Mardi Gras costumes and other glittering regalia. The museum's hours are Tuesday through Saturday from 9:00 A.M. until 5:00 P.M. and on Sundays from 3:00 until 5:00 P.M. Admission is modest. Call (318) 234–2208 for more information.

A walking tour from this point will take you past some of the city's landmark buildings including the **Cathedral of St. John the Evangelist,** an interesting structure of German-Romanesque design.

Either University Avenue or St. Mary Avenue, both of which turn off Lafayette Street, will lead you to the University of Southwestern Louisiana. Look for a parking place somewhere near the student union, then head for the tall cypress trees. Right in the middle of campus, you'll see an honest-to-goodness swamp studded with cypress trees trailing their streamers of Spanish moss. Called ◆**Cypress Lake**, the natural swamp (about the size of a city block) comes complete with native vegetation, waterfowl, migratory birds, fish, and even alligators.

Because this is a mini-swamp, you get a sense of the mysteries such an environment conceals—without the threat of danger. Visitors are welcome to stroll along the water's edge and feed the ducks. Small signs placed at intervals in the murky water invite you to PLEASE FEED THE FISH and inform you that this is an alligator habitat. (You're not supposed to feed the alligators, but, if you toss half a hot dog to the fish and it's intercepted by an alligator, it's best to let him have his way.)

A must-see in Lafayette is ◆**Acadian Village,** located on the southwest edge of town. After leaving the campus take Route 167 south until you reach Ridge Road, where you'll turn right. Next take a left on West Broussard Road. Then you'll follow the signs

Acadian Village

to Acadian Village. By the time you reach this cluster of buildings situated on a bayou and surrounded by gardens and woodlands, you'll agree it's definitely off the beaten path.

When you step through the gate, you may feel as if someone turned the calendar back about two hundred years. With its general store, schoolhouse, chapel, and original steep-roofed houses, the folklife museum replicates a nineteenth-century Acadian settlement.

Stop at the general store to buy a ticket and pick up a guide sheet describing the individual buildings. Strolling along a brick pathway and crossing wooden footbridges, you'll wend your way in and out of the various vintage structures. Although the blacksmith shop, chapel, and general store are reproductions, all other structures are authentic, most dating from the early 1800s. Transported from various locations throughout Acadiana, they were restored and furnished with native Cajun household items, clothing, photographs, books, and tools. The charming village captures the spirit of early Acadiana, and commercialism is noticeably absent.

The LeBlanc House, birthplace of Acadian state senator Dudley J. LeBlanc, contains a display featuring the tonic Hadacol. An early elixir touted to cure all ailments, this vitamin tonic concocted by LeBlanc, fondly known as "Couzan Dud," contained twelve percent alcohol. During the early 1950s George Burns, Bob Hope, Jack Benny, Mickey Rooney, Jimmy Durante, and other entertainers performed in Hadacol caravans, updated versions of the old-time traveling medicine shows.

The Billeaud House's exhibits focus on spinning and weaving. You'll see looms, spinning wheels, and a display of homespun coverlets and clothes. Take a look at the cotton patch, planted behind the cottage. If you packed a picnic, this peaceful setting is the perfect spot to enjoy it as you watch villagers (wearing the traditional clothing of their ancestors) spin wool on a porch or chat by the bayou.

Acadian Village is open daily from 10:00 A.M. to 5:00 P.M. The museum closes on New Year's Day, Mardi Gras Day, Easter Sunday, Thanksgiving, Christmas Eve, and Christmas Day. An admission fee is charged for adults and senior citizens, and children under six are admitted free. For exact directions or more information, call (318) 981–2364.

From Lafayette's outskirts it's only a fifteen-minute drive northeast via Route 94 to Breaux Bridge, also known as the Crawfish Capital of the World.

ST. MARTIN PARISH

If you visit ◆ **Mulate's Cajun Restaurant** at 325 Mills Avenue (on Route 94) in Breaux Bridge, owner Goldie Comeaux promises you a Cajun *"bon temps!"* Besides a good time, you can also anticipate good food. (You'll also find Mulate's restaurants in Baton Rouge and New Orleans.)

The restaurant's support beams came from cypress trees cut more than seventy years ago at the nearby swamp in Henderson. Local festival posters and paintings by Acadian artists line

Mulate's walls, and the tables are covered with red-and-white checkered cloths. Waiters speak both French and English.

Order some stuffed mushrooms or catfish tidbits to nibble on as you soak up some of the atmosphere, best described as lively and informal. While waiting for your entrée, you can take Mulate's Cajun quiz: "How to tell a full-blooded, dipped-in-the-bayous Cajun from someone who just wishes he was."

The restaurant offers dozens of fresh seafood dishes including catfish, shrimp, oysters, and frog legs. The dinner of stuffed crabs, also a house specialty, comes with jambalaya (jum-bo-LIE-ya), coleslaw, homemade French fries, and garlic bread. If you order the super seafood platter, you can sample stuffed crab, stuffed bell pepper, fried shrimp, catfish, oysters, frog legs, and jambalaya. Prices are moderate.

Authentic "chank-a-chank" music sends everybody, including children, to the dance floor. Parents holding toddlers in their arms waltz round and round or dance the Cajun two-step to the beat of triangles, fiddles, and accordions. The restaurant features live music at lunch on Saturday and Sunday and seven nights a week.

Open for breakfast Monday through Saturday, Mulate's hours are 7:00 A.M. to 10:30 P.M. daily and 11:00 A.M. to 11:00 P.M. on Sunday. Call (318) 332–4648 for information or reservations. Mulate's in-state toll-free number is 1–800–634–9880; outside Louisiana, call 1–800–42–CAJUN.

If you visit the Breaux Bridge area during the fall, you can watch sugar cane being harvested and hauled to market. This state produces much of America's sugar. (The sugar you spooned into your morning coffee or cereal may have come from South Louisiana's cane fields.) Harvesting starts in October, before winter's first freeze, and extends through late December. When the cane reaches a height of 9 to 11 feet, it is cut by mechanical harvesters and left in rows on the ground. Then the leaves are burned off, and the cane is loaded on trailers to be taken to nearby mills for processing. In this part of the country, you'll drive along roads strewn with stalks and pass many slow-moving trucks transporting their cargoes of cane from field to mill.

Only a few miles east of Breaux Bridge lies one of this country's great untamed regions, the **Atchafalaya Basin** (that large uncluttered area west of Baton Rouge on your state map). In this vast wilderness swamp, an overflow area for the Atchafalaya (a-CHOFF-a-lie-a) River, you can step back into a pristine world, but don't venture into its depths on your own. If you're game for a guided safari, take Route 347 northeast from Breaux Bridge, then pick up Route 352 to reach Henderson, the gateway to the Atchafalaya Basin. This area features a number of boat tours designed to introduce visitors to the Atchafalaya Basin's mysteries.

Driving through various portions of South Louisiana in the spring, you sometimes see people wading in ditches of water near the roadside. They are crawfishing—capturing those tasty little lobster look-alikes. Now that commercially grown crawfish is so readily available, this practice is not as common as it once was. Crawfishing is still great sport, however, and if you feel the urge to engage in this activity (children especially find it fascinating), it's a simple matter to buy some set nets, which cost about $1.00 each, at a local hardware store. Next find a nearby grocery store and buy some beef spleen, known as "melt," which usually runs about $1.00 per pound. Then, search out a deep ditch or swampy area. In this area of the state, you don't have to be a super sleuth to find one. Cut the meat into small pieces, and tie them to the centers of the nets. Spacing the nets several yards apart, place them in the water. After a few minutes grab a stick and start yanking the nets up, and presto!—dinner.

If you prefer someone else to snare and prepare your crawfish, head for Henderson and ❖ **Pat's Fisherman's Wharf Restaurant,** located on Route 352 across the bridge. Request to be seated on the porch, and you can look directly down into Bayou Amy.

Restaurant owner Pat Huval helped put Henderson on the map. After buying the restaurant in 1954, he added crawfish to the menu. (At that time, restaurants seldom served crawfish.) The specialty proved so popular that it created a new industry for the town—raising, processing, and selling crawfish.

Here is the place to sample Hank Williams's famed "jambalaya, crawfish pie, and filet gumbo," while a Cajun band provides listening entertainment. Be sure you're hungry because the meal starts with a salad and a cup of delicious gumbo (probably the state's most famous dish and often served with a dollop of rice). When my husband and I visited, the waitress brought gumbo for us, and she gave me some rice but left none for my husband.

Returning momentarily, she set down a bowl of rice, saying, "Here is for Papou" (pa-POO).

Afterward, a large platter (garnished with two bright red crawfish like miniature lobsters in armor) containing crawfish *étouffée,* fried crawfish, *boulette* (a fried crawfish meatball), and hush puppies, arrives.

If you don't want crawfish for dinner, a delicious alternative is Pat Huval's seafood platter, a house specialty featuring a green salad, seafood gumbo, fried shrimp, frog legs, oysters, catfish, french fries, and hush puppies. "Our food is so fresh," says Huval, "the catfish slept in the river last night." The restaurant is noted for its dirty rice (so called because it's cooked with chopped chicken giblets—not dropped on the floor). In season you can also order turtle soup. Rates are moderate. The restaurant is open daily from 10:00 A.M. until 11 P.M. Call (318) 228–7110.

For your excursion into the Atchafalaya, you can catch a boat tour at **McGee's Landing.** To get there head for Levee Road and turn left at the fourth exit. Just past Whiskey River landing, you'll see McGee's.

The two-hour tour takes you into a different world—a jungle of plants such as wild hibiscus, lotus, and elephant ears. Lots of trees also grow here—cypress, hackberry, willow, and oak, to name a few. The swamp serves as home to alligators, nutria, muskrats, minks, opossums, otters, ducks, turkeys, wading birds, and other wildlife. You'll glide under the Swampland Expressway, the 18-mile span on Interstate 10, which opened up Cajun country to the rest of the world. Building this bridge, once considered impossible because of the basin's boggy bottom, required considerable engineering ingenuity. If you encounter fog when driving on this stretch of interstate over the swamp, please exercise extreme caution. Heavy mists come with the terrain, and being suspended over a swamp magnifies the hazard.

For reservations at McGee's Landing, call (318) 228–2384. You can choose from a "Camera Eye" tour at 10:00 A.M., a "Daydreamer" tour at 1:00 P.M., or a "Lazy Daze" tour at 3:00 P.M. During summer months a "Sundowner" tour at 5:00 P.M. also is offered. Rates are reasonable. There's a $30.00 minimum cost per tour, so you may want to join another group.

From here head south toward St. Martinville. You can either return to Breaux Bridge by way of Route 347, which continues to

St. Martinville, or follow Route 31 south from Breaux Bridge. Another option is Route 96, an off-the-beaten-path road by way of Catahoula.

On the outskirts of St. Martinville in a serene park setting at 1200 North Main Street, you'll find the ◆ **Longfellow-Evangeline State Commemorative Area** on the banks of Bayou Teche. (The word *teche,* pronounced "tesh," comes from a Native American word meaning "snake" and refers to the bayou's serpentine path.)

This large complex offers facilities for boating, swimming, and picnicking. The park's main thrust, however, is to preserve and interpret the history of its early French settlers. Many Acadians who were forced by Britain to leave their Canadian "Acadie" in 1755 later made their way to South Louisiana. Henry Wadsworth Longfellow's epic poem *Evangeline,* the symbol of all Acadiana, tells the story of their long struggle to find a new home.

On the **Olivier Plantation,** an 1815 Creole raised cottage serves as the park's focal point and contains furnishings typical of that period. This plantation house and its detached kitchen, herb garden, and smokehouse, in a setting of ancient live oaks for which Cajun country is famous, present a living history lesson. Stop by the visitors' center for a look at the variety of exhibits related to early Acadian and Creole lifestyles. Except for Thanksgiving Day, Christmas Day, and New Year's Day, the park is open daily from 9:00 A.M. to 5:00 P.M. Admission is modest. Call (318) 394–3754 for more information.

Continue to the charming downtown area of "Le Petit Paris," as St. Martinville was once known. The town became a haven for aristocrats escaping the French Revolution's horrors during "the worst of times." Slave rebellions in the Caribbean sent other French planters here, and French Creoles from New Orleans joined them. With a patrician population prone to staging courtly ceremonies, elaborate balls, concerts, and operas, St. Martinville developed into a cultural mecca.

The mother church of the Acadians occupies a place of prominence on the ◆ **St. Martin de Tours Church Square.** Dating from 1832, the current structure contains some original sections from its 1765 predecessor—an altar, box pews, and chapel. Inside St. Martin de Tours Catholic Church are a silver and gold sanctuary light and carved marble baptismal font, said to be gifts from

Louis XVI and Marie Antoinette. Somewhat to the side and rear of the church, you'll see a statue of Evangeline, for which actress Dolores del Rio posed when she portrayed the heroine in an early movie filmed here. Movie cast members later presented the bronze monument to the townspeople.

Le Petit Paris Museum, constructed in 1861, stands on the right side of the church and contains local arts and crafts, church records, early documents, colorful carnival costumes, and Mardi Gras memorabilia. Except for major holidays, the museum is open daily from 9:30 A.M. to 4:30 P.M.

Church Square is also the setting for the Presbytère (priest's home), a beautiful white-columned structure built in 1856. Restored and furnished with period antiques, the home is open for tours by appointment only. For information on a guided tour of the Church Square on Main Street, call Le Petit Paris Museum at (318) 394-7334.

Within easy walking distance (a block or so) from Church Square, you'll see the **Evangeline Oak** on Bayou Teche's bank. Like Evangeline, many Acadian refugees in pursuit of their dreams stepped ashore at this spot. According to legend, Evangeline's boat docked under the large old tree when she arrived from Nova Scotia searching for her lover. Local lore differs from Longfellow's tale, but both stories portray the heartbreak of a forced exodus. Emmeline Labiche (Evangeline's real-life counterpart), after a ten-year search, discovered her true love, Louis Arceneaux (Gabriel in Longfellow's poem), here under the Evangeline Oak only to learn that he had since married another. It's said that Emmeline died of a broken heart, and the nearby Evangeline shrine marks her grave. (If oak trees could talk, this one might say that another tree actually witnessed the sad scene because *which* live oak is the authentic Evangeline Oak remains a topic of debate. This massive specimen nevertheless serves as a stately symbol.)

After exploring "Evangeline country," follow Route 31 south toward New Iberia.

VERMILION PARISH

Traveling southwest on Route 14 will take you to **Delcambre Shrimp Boat Landing,** located about 15 miles from New

Iberia. Known as the Shrimp Capital of Louisiana, the picturesque Acadian town of Delcambre stands with one foot in Vermilion Parish and the other in Iberia Parish.

At the fisherman's wharf you can hear Cajun French spoken and watch the day's catch being unloaded. You can also buy shrimp—fresh, frozen, cleaned, or the do-it-yourself kind—at any of the several seafood shops here and indulge in a shrimp feast at the covered picnic area nearby.

In August Delcambre hosts a four-day shrimp festival, which includes a blessing of the fleet. During shrimping season, generally from April through June and again from August through October, you'll see shrimp boats departing from Delcambre on their way to Vermilion Bay or the Gulf of Mexico. After harvesting their bounty the shrimp trawlers return to home port, their hulls filled with iced-down shrimp to be sorted, packed, and frozen. From this small inland port, millions of pounds of shrimp are shipped annually to both American and international markets.

Don't miss ◆ **Abbeville,** Vermilion's parish seat. This charming French-flavored town, which served as the setting for several movies, lies only a few miles west of Delcambre on Route 14. You'll find the beautiful Mary Magdalen Church built in 1910, lovely homes, and outstanding eateries such as Black's Oyster Bar and Bertrand's Riverfront Restaurant.

The town is also home to The Abbey Players, a local theater group that, in the words of resident Gerard Sellers, a documentary film maker, location scout, and performer himself, has a reputation for presenting polished performances and producing professional actors. You'll find The Abbey Theater, which is on the National Historic Register, at the corner of Lafayette and State streets. For information on performances, call (318) 893–2442.

Steen's Syrup Mill, located at Abbeville, is one of the nation's largest open-kettle syrup mills. Here, from mid-October through December, you can smell the sweet boiling cane syrup as raw sugar cane is converted into an amber-colored substance almost as thick as taffy. For more information on the area, call the Vermilion Parish Tourist Commission at (318) 898–4264.

For a unique gift or souvenir from Abbeville, consider one of Kathy Richard's Swamp Ivory Creations. Kathy, nicknamed "the head hunter," collects about 500 alligator skulls a year from a local processing plant and spreads them outside her studio to season. She later turns the alligator teeth into striking jewelry—earrings, pins, necklaces, and bolos. Nearby, Kathy's husband Johnny runs a saddle shop and does leathercrafting in an old livestock sale barn. To see his antique saddle collection and memorabilia or to visit Kathy's workshop, call (318) 893–5760.

In nearby Kaplan, Pat Herpin offers a service called TOUR MASTERS. Covering rural Acadiana, she arranges customized agriculture tours, aquaculture farm tours (alligator, crawfish, catfish), Cajun bush track racing outings, Cajun cooking demonstrations, and a sportsman's hunting or fishing package. For more information, call (318) 643–8481.

Afterward, return to Delcambre and take Route 675 north to Jefferson Island, about 10 miles west of New Iberia.

IBERIA PARISH

Jefferson Island is situated on a salt dome (the tip of a huge mountain of salt forced to the surface from deep within the earth) and is the setting for ◆**Live Oak Gardens.** You approach the site along a 2-mile drive lined with live oak trees. You can stroll through twenty acres of lovely landscaped gardens and tour an opulent home that stage actor Joseph Jefferson designed and had built in 1870.

Jefferson, one of America's most famous nineteenth-century actors, made a name for himself portraying Rip Van Winkle. He bought Jefferson Island to use as a winter retreat and hired French craftsmen from New Orleans to build the unique house with its elements of Moorish, Victorian gingerbread, and Steamboat Gothic architecture. Inside you'll see collections of crystal and porcelain, antiques, and paintings—including several local landscapes painted by the actor, who had a studio on the house's second floor.

It is said that Jefferson Island was one of pirate Jean Lafitte's hideouts, and the three pots of gold and silver coins discovered here in 1923 lend credibility to the rumor; the Lafitte Oaks mark the spot where the treasure was found. Footpaths lead to a rose garden, a Japanese garden, an Elizabethan knot garden featuring interlacing plants, and other beautifully landscaped areas.

A cafe on the grounds offers lunch selections, and you can sit at a table on the gallery and look across peaceful Lake Peigneur.

Live Oak Gardens

Tranquility, however, has not always been part of the picture. In 1980 a freak mining disaster violently rearranged the island's geography when a drilling rig punctured the salt dome under Lake Peigneur. The resulting maelstrom swallowed up the lake's contents—crewboats, barges, and all. An account of this cataclysmic event is part of a film on Jefferson Island's history, which visitors are shown when they tour **Live Oak Gardens.**

Except for major holidays, Live Oak Gardens can be visited seven days a week from 9:00 A.M. to 5:00 P.M. Winter hours are from 9:00 A.M. to 4:00 P.M. Tickets may be bought in the gift shop. For more information call (318) 365–3332.

From Jefferson Island continue on Route 675 into New Iberia, a Spanish stronghold in the midst of French territory. The town was named for Europe's Iberian Peninsula.

Don't miss ◆ **Shadows-on-the-Teche,** a white-pillared plantation house located at 317 East Main Street. Visitors park along a well-traveled street in front of the mansion. Once on the lovely grounds, however, one forgets traffic and other modern distractions. Statuary, camellias, wisteria, magnolia trees, and magnificent live oaks festooned with Spanish moss form a serene backdrop for Shadows-on-the-Teche. The mansion's name was inspired by the interplay of lights and darks across the lawn, created by sunlight filtering through the trees.

Built in 1834 for sugar planter David Weeks, the manor house stands on Bayou Teche's bank. (You don't see the bayou until you step into the backyard.) Slaves collected mud from the bayou's banks to make the house's coral-colored bricks. All the Shadows' main rooms open onto galleries, and there is no central hall. An exterior flight of stairs in front of the house, concealed by a lattice, leads to the second floor.

When William Weeks Hall (the original owner's great-grandson) took over the mansion during the early 1920s, he found it in an advanced state of deterioration. An artist, Hall lived in Paris before relocating to New Iberia to accept his lifetime challenge of restoring the Shadows to its former grandeur. Throwing himself into the restoration project, he also threw open his doors to extend Southern hospitality to such celebrities as Mae West, Henry Miller, W. C. Fields, and H. L. Mencken. In the pantry you'll see a door covered with signatures scribbled by Hall's houseguests—Cecil B. DeMille, Arleigh Burke, Tex Ritter, Walt Disney (along with his alter ego, Mickey Mouse) and others. Hall's friends referred to him as "the last of the Southern gentlemen."

Hall, who died in 1958, willed Shadows-on-the-Teche to the National Trust for Historic Preservation. When researchers discovered the mansion's original inventory of furnishings filed in an adjoining parish, they used it as a mandate to furnish the house as authentically as possible. The mansion's accessories include everything from indigo-dyed trousers and pier tables to finger bowls and foot warmers.

Except Thanksgiving Day, Christmas Day, and New Year's Day, the mansion is open daily from 9:00 A.M. until 4:30 P.M. Admission is modest. For additional information, call (318) 369–6446.

After touring the Shadows, plan to stop by **Lagniappe Too Cafe** for lunch. Located nearby at 204 East Main Street, this delightful little restaurant lives up to its name. Lagniappe translates to "a little something extra," which is exactly what you get at this eatery, owned by Elaine and Al Landry.

No matter which entrée you elect, you can't go wrong. I had the mirliton (a type of tropical squash) stuffed with shrimp and beef, and it was delicious. There's also an eggplant version; each comes with a salad, vegetables, and special Lagniappe bread rounds. Another popular item is the shrimp and avocado salad. Don't forgo dessert here. If you miss Tante Mouth's W. B. Bread Pudding (Elaine is on target when she says W. B. means "world's best"), you'll leave hating yourself. Al's original art, a feast for your eyes, lines the walls. Some works are serious and others whimsical.

Lagniappe Too serves lunch Monday through Friday and is open from 10:00 A.M. until 2:00 P.M. The cafe also serves dinner on Friday and Saturday from 6:00 to 9:00 P.M. For orders to go, call (318) 365–9419.

The **Estorge-Norton House,** a charming three-story structure of cypress that dates from about 1912, offers bed and breakfast accommodations. Located at 446 East Main Street in the heart of New Iberia's historic district, the home makes an ideal place to headquarter while taking in the local attractions, which should definitely include a walking tour of the historic district.

You can enjoy a full breakfast in the sun room, kitchen, or dining room. The downstairs area features an antique shop and even contains an elevator. Owner Charles Norton will make you feel right at home.

On the second floor a variety of accommodations are offered. Rates are standard to moderate. An apartment on the third floor sleeps four and offers a kitchen and private bath. House regulations request no smoking or pets. The home is closed during January, February, July, August, and part of September. For reservations call (318) 365–7603.

Plan to stop at nearby **Trappey's Factory and Cajun Shop,** located at 900 East Main Street. A short video acquaints you with Trappey's (tra-PAYS) history. Because gas escapes during the pepper-pickling process, try not to inhale too deeply because the fumes can overwhelm your senses. If you suffer from sluggish sinuses, however, this tour provides instant relief. It may also bring on a few therapeutic tears, but your tour guide will distribute tissue.

Save some time for browsing in Trappey's Cajun store because manager Mary Copas Segura selects and stocks unique items, some made by local artisans. You can surprise your friends at home with Cajun postcards made of native cypress wood. You can also find recipe books, chef's aprons, gift baskets, and cups ranging from novelty mugs to beautiful hand-painted demitasse sets. Chip dips made with hot sauces and cocktail wieners, which visitors may try, are prepared each day. You can also enjoy free coffee and have a go at Trappey's tasting table, set up with samples of Trappey's products. (My favorite was the pickled cocktail okra.) The company features a line of hot pepper and steak sauces. Before leaving be sure to notice the beautiful 300-year-old live oak on the grounds, a lovely spot for a picnic.

The Cajun store is open from 9:00 A.M. to 4:30 P.M. Monday through Saturday. Daily tours start at 9:00, 9:45, and 10:30 A.M. and again at 1:00, 1:45, and 2:30 P.M. Friday's last tour begins at 1:00 P.M. Admission is modest. Call (318) 365–8281 for more information.

At 309 Ann Street, you'll find the **Konriko Rice Mill and Company Store,** offering tasty treats and another interesting tour. Sip a cup of coffee while you watch a twenty-minute slide presentation on Cajun culture and the history of rice harvesting and milling. Afterward you can tour America's oldest working rice mill and browse in the Konriko Company Store (a replica of an actual company store). You might be given a rice cake to munch on and a sample of artichoke rice or other Konriko specialty. The store, which carries local foods, craft items, and gifts, is open Monday through Saturday from 9:00 A.M. until 5:00 P.M. Admission is modest. The number is 1–800–551–3245.

Before leaving New Iberia be sure to drive by the Iberia Savings Bank, located at 301 East St. Peter, to see the statue of Hadrian displayed on the bank's Weeks Street side. (Hadrian ruled the Roman Empire from A.D. 117 to 138.) Created by an unknown Roman sculptor around A.D. 130, the statue of white marble is 7 feet tall and weighs about 3,000 pounds. Originally the statue stood near the present site of a Rome railway station. In 1820 it was lugged from Italy to a castle in England, which served as the statue's home until 1961, when it was brought to New Iberia. A glass dome encloses the statue (which is spotlighted at night), and you can see it at any time.

From New Iberia it's only about 6 miles south on Route 329 to ◈**Avery Island** (actually a 5,000-acre salt dome). Chances are your kitchen cabinet already contains the island's famous export—Tabasco sauce. The red sauce comes in a small bottle for a very good reason—it is meant to be used sparingly, unless Cajun blood runs in your veins.

Not only is the sauce hot, but so is the temperature (most of the time) on this lush island, the home of the **McIlhenny Tabasco** factory. An introductory movie explains how Tabasco peppers are grown, aged, and made into the fiery sauce. The peppers are pulverized, put into huge vats, and covered with a thick layer of salt (which is mined in tunnels beneath the island's surface). After three years of fermentation, the mixture is diluted with salt and vinegar and then bottled. You can observe the bottling process from behind a glass window. You'll also receive a miniature bottle (the one-eighth-ounce size in such demand by airlines and restaurants that orders cannot be filled fast enough) of the celebrated hot pepper sauce to take back home. Free factory tours, which take about half an hour, are conducted Monday through Friday from 9:00 to 11:45 A.M. and from 1:00 to 3:45 P.M. Saturday hours are from 9:00 to 11:45 A.M.

After the factory tour, you can explore the island's 250-acre bird and animal sanctuary, **Jungle Gardens** (either by car or on foot). If you packed a lunch, head for the picnic tables under massive bearded live oak trees. You'll be entertained by prancing peacocks and nesting egrets against a backdrop of exotic vegetation from all over the world. Wasi orange trees, Chinese bamboo, South American papaya trees, and Egyptian papyrus all grow here as well as a profusion of other trees, shrubs, and blooming plants. Don't miss the ancient statue of Buddha, originally commissioned for a Chinese temple, sitting atop a lotus throne in a glass pagoda overlooking a lagoon.

Another must in this wildlife paradise is **Bird City,** one of the country's largest egret rookeries. During the latter part of the nineteenth century when the great demand for feathers to adorn women's hats almost led to the egret's extinction, conservationist Edward Avery McIlhenny (son of Tabasco's creator, Edmund McIlhenny) caught seven young egrets and raised them in a flying cage that he built on the island. The snowy egrets were later released to fly south for the winter, but they returned to Avery Island the next spring. And their descendants continue the practice—to the tune of some 20,000 birds each year.

Proceed on your safari with caution. Alligators slither all around. (How close they get is up to you.) They love to be tossed marshmallows (a practice frowned on by the management). To alligators, marshmallows look like egret eggs, and they gobble up both with gusto. Jungle Gardens can be visited seven days a week; hours are from 8:00 A.M. to 5:30 P.M. (until dark in summer). Admission fee is charged.

From Avery Island take Route 329 northeast to U.S. Highway 90 south and proceed to Franklin.

St. Mary Parish

Franklin, a lovely town founded in 1808, features several plantation homes as well as the nearby Chitimacha Indian Reservation. Settled mainly by Englishmen, the town (said to be the only one in the state that sided with the North during the Civil War) was named for Benjamin Franklin.

Located 5 miles northwest of Franklin off U.S. Highway 90 on Route 182, you'll find ✦ **Oaklawn Manor** at Irish Bend Road. The home was built in 1837 by Judge Alexander Porter, an Irish merchant who founded the state's Whig Party and also served as a United States senator.

Once the center of a large sugar plantation, the three-story Greek Revival house, which faces Bayou Teche, is splendidly furnished and contains many European antiques. Be sure to notice Judge Porter's original marble bathtub (to which a drain was later added). The house's bricks were made from clay on the premises. Magnificent live oaks and lovely gardens provide a perfect setting for the mansion, now occupied by State Senator and Mrs. Murphy J. Foster.

"We have oak trees that were here when Columbus discovered America," says guide Mamie Broussard. Black and white rabbits hop about on the grounds, and the nearby aviary is home to an assortment of birds, including fifteen parrots. Be sure to visit the mansion's original milk and butter house on the grounds.

Except for major holidays, Oaklawn is open daily (even on Mondays when many area plantations close) from 10:00 A.M. until 4:00 P.M. Admission is charged. For additional information call (318) 828–0434.

Continuing south on U.S. Highway 90 takes you to Morgan

City, a commercial fishing center. About 3 miles north of town on Route 70 at Lake Palourde, you'll find **Brownell Memorial Park,** a pleasant place to take a driving break. The Brownell Carillon Tower houses sixty-one bronze bells which chime every hour. The park offers picnicking facilities and is open daily from 9:00 A.M. to 5:00 P.M. Admission is free.

If you continue traveling southeast on U.S. Highway 90, you'll arrive in Houma, a perfect place to begin exploring the toe portion of Louisiana's boot.

SOUTHEAST LOUISIANA

Southeast Louisiana

Terrebonne Parish

Entering Terrebonne (TER-a-bone) Parish from the west, you'll take U.S. Highway 90 to reach Houma (HOME-uh). Between Morgan City and Houma, this road follows Bayou Black. Driving along you'll notice portions of the dark water covered by a bright green film. This substance, known as duckweed, may look like slime to you, but to ducks, it's dinner. A close examination of the plant reveals a mass of tiny four-petaled flowers. One of the world's smallest flowering plants, duckweed makes a tasty salad for ducks and geese.

Because of its many waterways, Houma is sometimes called the Venice of America. Its navigable bayous and canals serve as streets for shrimp boats and various vessels that glide by the town's backyards. The parish was established in 1834 on the banks of Bayou Terrebonne (which means "good earth"), and more than half of it is water. Houma is named for a Native American tribe that settled here during the early eighteenth century. Later Cajun settlers arrived and were joined by English, German, and Irish families.

A delightful way to acquaint yourself with the local flora and fauna is to take a swamp cruise, and the region offers several choices. For a swamp tour with a unique slant, try ◆ **A Cajun Man's Swamp Cruise,** headquartered at Bayou Black Marina on U.S. Highway 90, about 18 miles west of Houma and 20 miles east of Morgan City.

Black Guidry, a French-speaking Cajun singer who dishes up music with his commentary and tour, serves as captain for this trek into a beguiling wilderness. "Folks, if you want to know something, ask me," he says. "If I don't know the answer, I'll tell you a lie, and you won't know the difference." It's obvious that he knows this lush area well, and he often checks his crab traps along the way. Black sometimes brings along Gatorbait, his Catahoula cur. As is characteristic of his breed, Gatorbait is a patchwork of mottled colors—almost a genetic explosion, in fact. What Gatorbait lacks in beauty, he makes up for in personality, and his energetic approach to life makes any swamp cruise memorable.

Black will take you through a surrealistic world of cypress trees, adorned with swaying Spanish moss. You'll see elephant ears, palmettos, muscadine (wild grape) vines, and pretty purple hyacinths (which rob the water of oxygen and are extremely difficult to control). Black will point out bulrush, which provides nesting areas for snowy egrets, black-crowned night herons, and other birds. You'll probably see cormorants, ibis, blue herons, ducks, cranes, red-tailed hawks, and perhaps bald eagles and pelicans. You may also spot nutria (fur-bearing members of the rodent family), otters, turtles, snakes, alligators, and other creatures that populate this eerie realm.

Black's "pet" alligators recognize the sound of his boat and come when he calls (unless they're hibernating). Papa Gator, who is 14 feet long, and other members of his family may put in an appearance. According to Black, a couple of the smaller alligators are twins, and he named them the French equivalents of "ugly" and "lazy." Black rewards the alligators with treats. They prefer chicken, but they'll settle for catfish and even bakery products.

After the boat tour Black will play his guitar and sing for you. A gifted musician, he composes songs and appears on national television. Maybe he'll sing "Crawfish, Crawdads, Mudbugs, and Other Things" (from one of his albums) or a Hank Williams favorite like "Jambalaya," whose famous line "Son of a gun, we're gonna have big fun on the Bayou!" takes on added relevance in this setting.

During the musical session Black will show you his Cajun accordion made from part of a wooden chest, diaper pins, and other materials of opportunity. Cajuns are noted for their resourcefulness; they are also known for their friendliness, zest for life, strong family ties, and cooking skills. "Most Cajun men cook," says Black's wife, Sondra, "and are *good* cooks."

The swamp cruise, narrated in either French or English, takes about two hours and costs $15.00 per adult and $10.00 per child (ages three through twelve). Youngsters under three get free rides. Telephone ahead because tour times vary. For reservations call (504) 868–4625 or (504) 575–2315.

While in Cajun country try to take in a *fais-do-do* (FAY-doe-doe), a sort of Acadian hoedown with lots of dancing, talk, and laughter. Ask Sondra or Black about any local shindigs that may be going on. Houma's warm and friendly folks will make you

109

feel right at home. The Guidrys can also arrange crab, crawfish, or shrimp boils (in season) for tour groups of twenty or more.

If you're game for another tour, just across the road from the marina on Bayou Black Road (parallel to U.S. Highway 90), you'll find **Wildlife Gardens.** Owned by Betty and James Provost, the preserve is populated with some 500 animals from South Louisiana. The Provosts' pets range from beavers, bobcats, raccoons, and deer to ducks and rare black swans. The natural swamp setting in Gibson is also home to great horned owls, pheasants, exotic chickens, alligators, and alligator loggerhead turtles.

Here you can give bread to the white-tailed deer, perhaps scratch their velveteen horns, and watch their fawns being bottle-fed. Be careful not to step on Jill, a pot-bellied pig with a penchant for following people around. Watch out for Clarence, a ninety-pound alligator loggerhead turtle and Big Ben, a century-old loggerhead who's even larger. The Provosts also operate an alligator farm, and visitors can touch the babies and observe the different stages of alligator growth.

On a guided tour, you'll see an authentic trapper's cabin with furnishings. A gift shop on the premises sells native crafts including James's handcarved duck decoys and a selection of unique jewelry that Betty makes from alligator buttons (vertebrae) and garfish scales. Except for Sundays and major holidays, tours are given daily at 10:00 A.M. and at 1:00 and 3:30 P.M. Admission is charged.

The Provosts also offer bed and breakfast. "Guests can stay in one of our three little cabins nestled in the swamp, very rustic and along the bayou," says Betty, "and can even paddle their own pirogue [docked outside] down the canal." Standard rates. For more information, call (504) 575–3676.

After your encounter with the local wildlife, continue on U.S. Highway 90 east to Houma. At 809 Bayou Black Drive, you'll find one of Black Guidry's favorite hangouts, ◆ **A-Bear's Cafe.** Owner Jane Hebert (pronounced "a-bear" in this area) , assisted by family members, dishes up some good Cajun cooking here. Her hearty breakfasts, popular with the local crowd, feature homemade biscuits, eggs, grits, and a choice of sausage, ham, or bacon.

The cafe's best-selling lunch is sausage, red beans, and rice with potato salad. Another delicious entrée is catfish A-Bear, a fried fillet of catfish topped with homemade crab sauce. This meal comes with a salad, gumbo, white beans, French bread, and pie. Prices are economical. Mr. Hebert's homemade lemon meringue and coconut pies will make you forget your diet. His pecan, pumpkin, and sweet potato pies are also great hits with the restaurant's customers.

Closed on Sunday, A-Bear's Saturday hours are 10:30 A.M. to 2:00 P.M. The weekday schedule runs from 7:00 A.M. to 5:00 P.M. except on Friday when the cafe also is open from 6:00 to 10:00 P.M. for dinner and musical entertainment provided by Black and Sondra Guidry. Their repertoire includes Black's original compositions, Cajun folk songs, and old favorites. People also bring their own instruments and join in the fun. Call (504) 872–6306.

While in Houma, take time to drive along Route 311 on the city's western outskirts to see several lovely plantation homes situated along Little Bayou Black.

Stop by ◆ **Southdown Plantation House,** located about 3 miles southwest of town on the corner of Route 311 and St. Charles Street. This grandiose pink Victorian mansion, trimmed in green, also serves as the Terrebonne Museum. Inside the twenty-one-room structure on the first floor, you'll see a colorful Mardi Gras exhibit. Be sure to notice the hall doorways with inserts of stained glass in a sugar cane motif.

Other interesting displays include an exhibit on Cajun history and a large collection of Boehm and Doughty porcelain birds. You'll also see a re-creation of the Washington, D.C., office of the late Allen J. Ellender from Houma, who served almost thirty-six years in the U.S. Senate. Autographed pictures of familiar political personalities line the wall. Senator Ellender's colleagues acknowledged him as the Senate's Master Chef, and his original gumbo recipe is still prepared in the U.S. Senate dining room. You can pick up a brochure featuring some of Senator Ellender's Creole recipes such as gumbo, shrimp Creole, jambalaya, oyster stew, and pralines.

Guided tours last about an hour and a half, and the day's last tour starts at 3:00 P.M. Except for holidays, Southdown is open daily from 10:00 A.M. to 4:00 P.M. Admission is modest. Call (504) 851–0154.

At this point, anglers might want to venture south on State Route 56 to Cocodrie. At ◆ **Coco Marina,** about 26 miles below

Houma, Johnny Glover promises good fishing year-round at his facility on the Gulf of Mexico's fruitful fringes. Here you can charter a boat (the marina currently operates seven boats, ranging from 25 to 31 feet in size) for fishing expeditions. A day's catch might include black drum, redfish, speckled trout, sheepshead, cobia, red snapper, flounder, and mackerel. The marina has recorded daily catches of more than twenty-six different species, and a typical weekend haul might bring in a sampling of ten to fifteen species.

Celebrate your catch at the **Island Oasis Bar** while enjoying a wetlands sunset. Afterward, you can dine at the Lighthouse Restaurant, which offers seafood specialties such as gumbo, blackened fish, and Wine Island shrimp. Or you can feast on your own catch in the privacy of your condo. The complex offers accommodations from motel units to studio apartments, and all buildings stand on 12- to 14-foot pilings. Except for Thanksgiving, Christmas Day, and New Year's Day, the marina is open daily. Rates are standard to moderate. Call 1–800–648–2626 or (504) 594–6626.

Afterward, return to Houma and follow Route 24 east until you reach Route 1 in Lafourche Parish. Then head south on Route 1, which runs parallel with Bayou Lafourche, known locally as the "longest street in the world." This waterway, busy with the traffic of barges, shrimp boats, and a variety of other vessels, extends to the Gulf of Mexico. A number of Cajun fishing communities line the shore.

Slow down when you reach the little town of Golden Meadow (actually you should slow down before you get here because the speed limit means what it says). Watch for a small shrimp boat, the *Petit Caporal,* moored beside Route 1. Named for Napoleon Bonaparte, the century-old boat serves as a monument to the area's shrimping industry.

While in Golden Meadow you'll also want to stop at **Dufrene's Bakery,** right on Route 1, where you can buy some of the best French bread in Louisiana. With your loaf of crusty bread and a sack of delicious pastries, you have a good start on the makings of a picnic, which you can later enjoy when you reach the beach. Driving through the area south of Golden Meadow and all the way down to the coast, you'll see a variety of birds—gulls, terns, shorebirds, and such.

Shrimp Boats

JEFFERSON PARISH

Located on the Gulf of Mexico at the end of Route 1, you'll discover ◆**Grand Isle.** A bridge links the narrow 8-mile barrier island to the mainland. You'll drive by fishing camps, homes built on tall pilings, and stretches of empty beaches. Grand Isle is noted for its excellent bird-watching, especially during spring and fall when migrating flocks follow the flyway (the migratory interstate for birds from Canada to Mexico), which crosses the island.

Grand Isle State Park, at the island's eastern tip, offers many seashore recreation opportunities such as fishing, surfing, crabbing, picnicking, and camping. A swimming beach, nature center observation platform, and fishing jetties also attract vacationers. Be sure to bring along your fishing gear because you can catch some big fish from the park's 400-foot pier. The superb fishing brings many folks this far off the beaten path. Grand Isle is also a headquarters for charter boats and deep-sea fishing. (Both a regular and a saltwater fishing license are required if you fish in Louisiana's coastal waters.) Park hours are 6:00 A.M. to 10:00 P.M. April 1 through Labor Day and 8:00 A.M. to 7:00 P.M. the remainder of the year. Call (504) 787–2559.

You'll have to return north after you've finished fishing and sunning because Grand Isle is the end of the line.

LAFOURCHE PARISH

At Golden Meadow once more, you can vary your route by switching from Route 1 to Route 308 (which also runs parallel with the waterway) on the eastern bank of Bayou Lafourche. Continue driving north toward Thibodaux (TIB-a-doe). Two miles before reaching Thibodaux, just off Route 308 on Route 33, you'll find **Laurel Valley Plantation.** Dating from the 1840s, this complex is America's largest surviving sugar plantation. Head first for the General Store and Museum where you'll see a couple of locomotives, old machinery, and a pen filled with chickens, ducks, sheep, and goats. The store carries prints depicting Laurel Valley Plantation as it looked during the nineteenth century, as well as local arts and crafts. You'll also see vintage items: iron pots, churns, crocks, smoothing irons, and farm implements. Laurel Valley Village consists of some seventy weathered structures including a manor house, school, blacksmith shop, and barns. A cane-lined drive takes you past rows of workers' cabins.

After leaving Laurel Valley drive on into Thibodaux (about five minutes away) to see the town's fine group of Victorian homes and other interesting buildings such as the courthouse, St. Joseph's Catholic Church, and St. John's Episcopal Church. The latter, dating from 1844, is the oldest Episcopal church west of the Mississippi River. Nearby **Nicholls State University** also features an interesting boat-building facility. After touring Thibodaux take Route 308 north toward Napoleonville.

ASSUMPTION PARISH

About 2 miles south of Napoleonville, a town founded by a former soldier of the Little Corporal, you'll find ♦**Madewood.** Dating from the 1840s, this magnificent white-columned Greek Revival mansion features a huge ballroom, handsome walnut staircase, and ornate plasterwork. The home is furnished with period antiques, fine paintings, Oriental rugs, and crystal chandeliers.

"We're the least commercial of the area plantations," says Keith Marshall, "and some of our guests have returned four and five times." He and his wife, Millie, make their lovely plantation home on Bayou Lafourche available for both day tours and overnight lodging. On the grounds you'll see an interesting old cemetery, several plantation outbuildings, and lovely landscaping complete with live oak trees and swaying Spanish moss.

Overnight guests are greeted with wine and cheese. A house tour, an elegant dinner (complete with candlelight and wine) followed by after-dinner coffee and brandy in the parlor, and a full plantation breakfast are included in the price of a mansion room or the nearby raised bay cottages. Rates are deluxe. With the exceptions of Thanksgiving, Christmas Day, and New Year's Day, Madewood is open daily from 10:00 A.M. to 5:00 P.M. Admission is charged. Call 1–800–749–7151 or (504) 369–7151 for reservations.

Depending on your time frame and interests, you can travel farther east to do some plantation hopping along the Great River Road (actually composed of several state highways) which parallels both sides of the Mississippi River between New Orleans and Baton Rouge. Along the way you'll see lovely scenery—magnolia, oak, pecan, and willow trees and many of the South's most beautiful plantation homes. Several of the plantation homes are patterned after Greek temples and feature long oak-lined approaches. Many of these magnificent old mansions offer both tours for daytime visitors and bed and breakfast accommodations for overnight guests.

Among the homes you can visit along River Road are Destrehan Manor, the oldest surviving plantation in the lower Mississippi Valley; San Francisco with its elaborate Steamboat Gothic design; the classic Houmas House, which served as a setting for many movies, including *Hush, Hush, Sweet Charlotte;* and the impressive Oak Alley with its grand canopy of live oak. But the biggest plantation house of all is Nottoway, located in Iberville Parish.

IBERVILLE PARISH

Nottoway (as well as several other great plantation homes) can be visited via steamboat on the Mississippi River. Nottoway visitors who use this mode of transportation simply walk across the levee and through the gate to the mansion's front door. If you wish to arrive in this grand manner, you have to climb aboard in New Orleans. (For information on excursions, refer to the section on the Delta Queen Steamboat Company described near the end of this chapter, see page 146.)

To visit Nottoway by car, take Route 1 north to Donaldsonville after leaving Madewood. Continue driving north until you reach White Castle, and then go north 2 more miles.

Nottoway, sometimes called The White Castle, is a splendid interpretation of the Italianate style. The three-story mansion with sixty-four rooms, once the centerpiece of a 7,000-acre plantation, was designed by acclaimed architect Henry Howard. Sugar baron John Hampden Randolph commissioned the house, which was completed in 1859. The 53,000-square-foot home provided plenty of space for the Randolphs' eleven children, staff, and visitors. Cornelia, one of the Randolph daughters, wrote a book about life at Nottoway entitled *The White Castle of Louisiana.* You can buy a copy at the gift shop.

Nottoway is now owned by Paul Ramsay of Sydney, Australia. Perhaps the home's ornate interior, the setting for exquisite antiques and art, is best exemplified by the grand White Ballroom. This immense room, with its white marble fireplace and Corinthian columns, is a vision in varying shades of white. With its gleaming floor (covered by three layers of white enamel), vanilla-colored walls, and lofty ceiling, this room made an elegant backdrop for both balls and weddings. Six of the Randolph daughters were married in the White Ballroom, and during the past decade some 500 weddings have also been performed here.

At Nottoway, unlike some mansions, visitors are told they may explore after the tour and go through any door that's not locked. Overnight guests are free to stroll through the mansion after hours.

If you're staying overnight, sherry and nuts are brought to your room before dinner. Dinner may be served either in Randolph Hall, an elegant restaurant on the grounds, or in the mansion's first-floor Magnolia Room (formerly a three-lane bowling alley original to the house).

Nottoway's food ranks in the superb category, thanks to chef Johnny Percle, who will astound you with his creative cookery. For dinner you may want to try the smoked and grilled quail, served on a nest of jambalaya with a vegetable, house salad, and homemade bread. I had blackened catfish, and it was delicious. Desserts range from chocolate chocolate (that's double chocolate) torte and cheesecake *du soir* to apple walnut pie and Bailey's Irish Cream mousse.

Overnight guests receive a wake-up call on the intercom and a prebreakfast pot of coffee, juice, and tasty sweet potato muffins delivered on a silver platter. Afterward they can enjoy a full plantation breakfast. The Ten Pin Alley breakfast menu features seasonal fresh fruit and a choice of entrées. The *pain perdu* (thick slices of French bread battered, buttered, fried, and sugared) with country sausage is scrumptious. Other choices include plantation waffles or a traditional breakfast of ham or sausage, with eggs, toast, and grits.

Nottoway is open daily for lunch from 11:00 A.M. until 3:00 P.M. and for dinner from 6:00 to 9:00 P.M. Nottoway closes at 3:00 P.M. on Christmas Eve and reopens on December 26. Otherwise, the mansion can be visited daily from 9:00 A.M. to 5:00 P.M. Admission is charged. For meal or room reservations, call (504) 346–8263 or (504) 545–2730. Rates are moderate to deluxe.

When you leave Nottoway (assuming you arrived by car instead of boat), you will exit near the gift shop. To see the world's smallest church (quite a contrast to the South's largest mansion), turn left when you drive out of Nottoway's parking lot. This puts you on Route 405, also called River Road, which runs in front of the mansion and beside the levee. Proceed toward Bayou Goula and watch for the ◆ **Chapel of the Madonna** on the left. (My car clocked the distance at 4.3 miles.) A green sign on the road's right side announces: SMALLEST CHURCH IN THE WORLD/MADONNA CHAPEL Unfortunately there's no place to park except on the roadside in front of the church, but at the time of my visit some members of a utility crew at work nearby assured me that this was quite all right.

You may feel a bit like Gulliver approaching a Lilliputian chapel as you open the gate of the fence surrounding this miniature church, which is about the size of a large closet. Mounted on the wall to the right of the door, you'll see a wooden box, which should contain a key to unlock the front door. If the key is not there, check the top of the door frame.

When I visited, several candles were burning, and three straight wooden chairs flanked each side of the altar. I was told that the church was built in 1890 by a devout woman to fulfill a vow she had made during her daughter's critical illness. An annual mass is held here on August 15. You can sign a register and make a donation if you wish.

After this brief detour return to Route 1 (there's a cut-through near Bayou Goula) and head north toward Baton Rouge. A few miles north you may want to stop in downtown Plaquemine to see the locks, built in 1900, which once provided the only access to waterways west of the Mississippi. **Plaquemine Locks** (no longer in use) linked the navigable Bayou Plaquemine with the Mississippi River. Here you'll see the original lockhouse with exhibits on the river's traffic and history. The facility also features picnic grounds and an observation tower that affords a sweeping view of the Mississippi River. After visiting Plaquemine continue to Baton Rouge, about 15 miles north.

EAST BATON ROUGE PARISH

According to legend Baton Rouge's name came from a notation on a map used by French explorer Pierre le Moyne, sieur d'Iberville, and his brother, Jean Baptiste le Moyne, sieur de Bienville, who led an expedition up the Mississippi River in 1699. Iberville spotted a tall cypress pole smeared with animals' blood, which apparently marked the dividing line between the hunting grounds of the Bayou Goula and Houmas Native American tribes who shared this area. When Iberville jotted *"le bâton rouge"* (French for "red stick") on his map, little did he know that he had named what would become Louisiana's capital city.

Baton Rouge offers many attractions, but most of them hardly qualify as off the beaten path, particularly the State Capitol or a major college campus like Louisiana State University. You'll miss some unique places, however, if you bypass them. Many of the city's historic sites are clustered close to the State Capitol, which stands on the north side of the downtown area. You can't miss it—it's thirty-four stories high, the tallest state capitol in the United States. The observation tower on the twenty-seventh floor affords a panoramic view of the city. A special project of Governor Huey P. Long, the Capitol was completed in 1932. (Ironically Long was later shot on the first floor of this building.)

Don't miss the Old State Capitol, which Mark Twain called "an atrocity on the Mississippi." Located at 100 North Boulevard, this Gothic Revival castle is currently undergoing renovation and will house Louisiana's Center for Political and Governmental History. You may also want to visit the U.S.S. *Kidd,* a World War II destroyer, located downtown on the riverfront at the foot of Government Street.

After your downtown sightseeing tour, head toward the city's southwestern corner for a visit to Louisiana State University. LSU offers interesting attractions ranging from museums and a live Bengal tiger to Indian mounds and a Greek amphitheater. You'll find the campus 1.5 miles south of downtown Baton Rouge, between Highland Road and Nicholson Drive.

Stop first at the Visitor Information Center, located on the corner of Dalrymple Drive and Highland Road, where you can pick up a parking permit (required Monday through Friday) and a campus map. Consider headquartering at nearby ◆ **Pleasant Hall,** which offers attractive accommodations at reasonable rates. This campus hotel, also the Continuing Education Center, makes a handy base within easy walking distance of LSU attractions and several eateries. A local dining guide is available at the lobby desk.

The concierge level offers lovely suites, decorated in French Colonial style, along with complimentary continental breakfast and evening snack. Rooms and suites come with private baths, cable TV, telephones, and daily maid service plus convenient parking. Also, guests may use the university's facilities such as the library, golf course, pool, and tennis courts. Rates are standard. For more information, call (504) 387–0297.

119

While on campus, stop by the **LSU Faculty Club** for lunch. Located on Highland Road across from the Parade Ground, the eatery is housed in an attractive building reminiscent of a French salon. The Faculty Club offers soups, salads, and sandwiches along with seafood, chicken, beef, and pasta entrées and desserts in an attractive setting, enhanced by live piano or harp music. Popular choices include the shrimp salad, gourmet burger, or glazed crab meat sandwich on an English muffin with cheese and fruit. Serving hours are Monday through Friday from 11:30 A.M. to 1:30 P.M.

Afterward you can visit Memorial Tower, built in 1923 as a monument to Louisianians who died in World War I. Housed in the tower, the **LSU Museum of Art** features a series of furnished rooms illustrating early English and American interiors. Various exhibits demonstrate England's enduring contribution to American culture. Among the museum's holdings are a number of impressive collections ranging from the seventeenth to mid-nineteenth centuries including several etchings and engravings by English artist William Hogarth. Also housed here are the largest public collection of New Orleans-made nineteenth-century silver, a fine Newcomb crafts collection, and a comprehensive grouping of prints—dating from 1932 to 1980—by internationally acclaimed Louisiana printmaker, Caroline Durieux. While on campus, inquire about current shows because the LSU Museum of Art and Hill Memorial Library sometimes sponsor joint exhibitions.

Admission to the museum is free; you can either browse on your own or take a group tour for a modest fee. Except for holidays, the museum is open from 9:00 A.M. to 4:00 P.M., Monday through Friday. On Saturday you can visit from 10:00 A.M. to noon and 1:00 to 4:00 P.M. Sunday hours are 1:00 to 4:00 P.M. Call (504) 388-4003 for more information on the museum.

Afterward you can stroll to nearby Foster Hall, home of the Museum of Natural Science, to see dioramas depicting Louisiana's wildlife. On display are mounted specimens of birds, reptiles, and animals, including LSU's original Bengal tiger mascot. (You also can visit the current mascot, Mike IV, who resides in an environmentally controlled home outside Tiger Stadium—a nearby sign reads GEAUX TIGERS!)

Before leaving campus make a point of seeing the 3,500-seat Greek amphitheater; the avenue of stately oak trees, planted as

memorials for LSU alumni killed in World War II; and two intriguing Indian mounds believed to date from 3300 to 3800 B.C.

A short distance northwest of the campus, you'll find ❖ **Magnolia Mound**, one of the state's oldest plantations. Located at
2161 Nicholson Drive, this 1791 home serves as a lovely example
of French Creole architecture. Surrounded by a grove of live oak
and magnolia trees, the house stands on a ridge facing the Mississippi levee.

Magnolia Mound, authentically restored, is made of large
cypress timbers joined by wooden pegs and packed with *bousillage*. Be sure to notice the quaint iron latches and the carved
woodwork. In the dining room you'll see an unusual buffet with
locked wine compartments and a Napoleon mirror over the man-
tel. Other interesting furnishings include an overseer's desk in
the plantation office, a pianoforte in the parlor, and an old rope
bed. According to the museum's guide, the familiar expression
"Good night; sleep tight" originated because some old-fashioned
beds used rope-supported mattresses that had to be pulled taut
periodically. Mattresses made with Spanish moss were used on
plantation beds during summer months and were replaced by
feather mattresses for winter.

On the grounds you'll see both a kitchen garden and a crop
garden and several outbuildings typical of early plantation life—a
detached kitchen, a pigeonnier, and an overseer's house.

Quilting exhibits, holiday candlelight tours, and weekly open-
hearth cooking demonstrations are scheduled to acquaint visitors with the lifestyle of colonial Louisiana. Magnolia Mound
opens at 10:00 A.M. Tuesday through Saturday and at 1:00 P.M.
on Sunday. The day's last tour starts at 3:30 P.M. The museum
closes on Mondays and holidays. Admission is modest. Call
(504) 343–4955.

Afterward, take time to drive along Highland Road, a scenic
byway. ❖ **Mount Hope Plantation** at 8151 Highland offers a
lovely interlude for travelers. After a tour of Ann and Jack Dease's
circa 1817 plantation home and gardens (where Confederate
troops camped), one can take a tea break. Helen Alexander, Ann's
sister, serves an array of tempting treats from English scones with
lemon curd, Devonshire cream, and fresh fruit preserves, to tea
sandwiches and homemade pastries—all beautifully presented.
Downstairs rooms feature charming tea settings amidst the

home's antique furnishings. Tea is served from 10:00 A.M. to 3:00 P.M. Rates are moderate. Mount Hope also offers bed and breakfast accommodations. For reservations, call (504) 766–8600.

If you want to step back into the past century, drive to the junction of Interstate 10 and Essen Lane, where you'll find the entrance to an outdoor complex called ◆ **Rural Life Museum.**

The museum's grounds occupy part of a family plantation that Steele Burden and his sister Ione Burden donated to Louisiana State University in 1965. The 450-acre tract serves as a setting for the museum as well as an agricultural research station.

The folk museum consists of more than fifteen old buildings collected from farms and plantations throughout the state. Instead of a "big house" (most farm families could not afford extravagant residences), you'll see a brick-front overseer's cottage with a parlor, dining room, and two bedrooms. The rooms are furnished with authentic utilitarian pieces. Nearby stands a kitchen, detached from the main house because of the danger of fire.

A row of slave cabins and other rustic buildings paint a picture of austerity. In the sick house, the plantation's infirmary, you'll see rope beds, a tooth extractor (circa 1800), and a shock-treatment machine from the 1850s (which generated mild electrical charges for treating arthritis, nervous twitches, and other ailments).

You can also visit a commissary, smokehouse, schoolhouse, blacksmith's shop, gristmill, cane grinder, and sugarhouse. Other structures include a country church, pioneer's cabin, corncrib, potato house, shotgun house, Acadian house, and dogtrot house. The museum's big barn contains hundreds of items including a voodoo exhibit, a 1905 Edison phonograph, plantation bells, bathtubs, irons, ox carts, trade beads, an African birthing chair, and pirogues.

The guided tour takes from one to two hours. The museum, open from 8:30 A.M. to 4:00 P.M. Monday through Friday, operates on Louisiana State University's schedule and closes on weekends and holidays. A modest admission is charged; call (504) 765–2437.

To see an impressive collection of European antiques and architectural elements, head for ◆ **Fireside Antiques** at 14007 Perkins Road. Owner Cheri McDaniel makes scouting expeditions to Europe in search of antique interiors such as rare French wall paneled rooms, doors, mantels, cornices, and other architectural elements from historical structures. A Baton Rouge builder whose own "new French chateau" incorporates authentic antique architectural details and furnishings, Cheri is also grandmother to Louisiana's first quadruplets. She took over Fireside Antiques, co-owned with her daughter, Susan Roland, after the babies brought on a career change for Susan.

At Fireside, you'll see such pieces as French Louis XV buffets, sleigh beds, cupboards, and consoles. The shop also adapts antique beds, such as Louis XV and XVI styles, to today's popular king and queen sizes. English mahogany and oak chairs, tables, servers, chests, stools, and benches are also on display as well as country pine tables, Welsh dressers, and single- or double-door armoires. Accessories range from stone garden urns to vases, teapots, and dried roses.

One of the shop's elegant showrooms provides an appropriate backdrop for tea. You can admire antique groupings while lingering over a pot of tea accompanied by scones, finger sandwiches, tea breads, truffles, and assorted pastries. Afternoon tea is served Tuesday through Saturday from noon to 3:30 P.M. Rates are moderate. Shop hours are Monday through Saturday from 10:00 A.M. to 5:30 P.M. Call 1–800–259–9565 or (504) 752–9565.

Afterward, follow U.S. Highway 190 west to Livonia and into French plantation country.

POINTE COUPEE PARISH

Don't miss ◆Joe's "Dreyfuss Store" Restaurant on State Route 77 south in Livonia. Bright, noisy, and popular, this jeans-and-Keds kind of place offers creative Creole cuisine in an old general store/pharmacy. The interior features displays of old-fashioned pharmaceutical products and nostalgic items, and Cream of Wheat posters line the walls. Try the marinated crab claws or turtle soup *au sherry*. Other specialties include crawfish entrées (seasonal), angel hair pasta with shrimp and crab meat, stuffed eggplant, crab and spinach *au gratin,* and pork loin. For dessert, order the bread pudding with rum sauce. Prices are moderate. Restaurant hours are Tuesday through Saturday from 11:00 A.M. to 2:00 P.M. and 5:00 to 9:00 P.M. Closed Sunday evening and on Monday. Call (504) 637–2625.

Afterward, follow State Route 78 north until it intersects State Route 1. You'll take a left here for ◆New Roads, but first turn right to visit **La Villa de Mon Coeur** (The House of My Heart) at 7739 False River Drive (State Route 1) about 8 miles south of New Roads. Mary Lou and Gene Perkins welcome visitors to their home, Mon Coeur, for tours and English afternoon tea. Business partner Dianne Jarreau, who brings her British background to this endeavor, says, "You come as visitors and leave as friends." Mary Lou and Dianne add a different twist to tea—a wardobe of hats. Each guest is encouraged to select and don a hat that fits her personality. While deciding on a garden party or plume-drooping version, pillbox or beret, most guests dissolve into laughter. By the time scones, gingerbread, and lemon curd arrive, everyone is sipping tea and sharing anecdotes. The full tea continues with finger sandwiches, such as cucumber and egg confetti, followed by cream horns and other pastries. Those who fancy spirits and libations can supplement their repast with wine, sherry, champagne, or a mint julep. By the way, Mary Lou and Diane adore having men as tea guests.

After tea, you can stroll in the gardens, designed by Steele Burden, or browse through Memories of Mon Coeur, a gift shop featuring antiques, Victorian linens, old books, and work by local artisans. Gift shop and tour hours are Wednesday through Saturday from noon to 4:00 P.M. Tea is served on Friday and Saturday from noon to 4:00 P.M. Rates are moderate. For reservations call (504) 638–4334 or (504) 638–7557.

Nearby **Parlange Plantation,** on State Route 1 just north of the State Route 78 intersection, makes another interesting stop in the New Roads area. A National Historic Landmark, this two-story galleried West Indies-type home built by the Marquis Vincent de Ternant dates to 1750. A working plantation of 2,000 acres, Parlange is still home to descendants of the original family. On a house tour, you'll see eight generations of family possessions, rare antique furnishings, china, and crystal. The main salon features unusual corner-hung family portraits. The guide will tell you about one forebear, Virginie (Mme. Pierre Gautreau), who posed for John Singer Sargent's then-startling *Portrait of Madame X* now housed in New York's Metropolitan Museum of Art. A house tour includes the wine cellar, which contains wooden brick molds used in the home's construction, and pigeonniers flanking the entrance. Parlange opens daily at 9:30

Parlange Plantation

A.M., and the last tour starts at 4:30 P.M. Admission is charged. Call (504) 638–4334.

Continue north to the charming town of New Roads on the bank of False River, an oxbow lake created when the Mississippi River changed its course during the 1700s. At 401 Richey Street you'll find **Pointe Coupee Bed and Breakfast** housed in two historical structures on an acre block. Owners Sidney and Al Coffee (a former LSU football player and sprinter) make guests feel at home in their 1902 Victorian Hebert House and the neighboring Sampson-Claiborne House, an 1835 Creole cottage; both homes feature rooms or suites with fireplaces, antique furnishings, and private baths. Breakfast starts with fruit and a sweet, perhaps mini-apple turnovers. Afterward, Sidney might serve a baked omelet with cheese, smothered potatoes, and homemade banana and pumpkin breads. Rates are standard to moderate.

The Coffees also offer candlelight dinners, complete with gourmet menu, wine, and soft music on request. For rates and reservations, call 1–800–832–7412 or (504) 638–6254. Sidney, who runs a cultural tour company called "Louisiana Backroads," shares her travel expertise with guests.

After exploring Pointe Coupee Parish, head for the St. Francisville Ferry. Except for the period between midnight and 4:00 A.M., the ferry makes four crossings an hour. While waiting, you'll see people standing around chatting or perhaps an enterprising youngster going from car to car selling bags of parched peanuts.

WEST FELICIANA PARISH

After crossing the Mississippi River, follow the ferry road (State Route 10, which soon becomes Ferdinand Street) up a hill into St. Francisville, a picturesque town in a tranquil setting of live oak, magnolia, and pine trees. A fascinating place to visit, this quaint village retains its nineteenth-century charm. Many plantation houses, built during the early 1800s, lie tucked away in the surrounding countryside.

About a mile from the ferry, you'll see a sign for the ◆ **Shade Tree** on your right. Perched on a hill at the corner of Ferdinand and Royal streets, the shop offers antiques, custom willow furniture, home and garden accessories, folk art, candles, handmade pottery, blown glassware, imported woven fabrics, hand-forged iron items, old tools, pocket knives, crystals, geodes, and other minerals. You'll also find wind chimes, baskets, prints, toys, willow and cypress bird feeders, books, gourmet coffees and teas, and jewelry. Be sure to notice a locally made line of bracelets and earrings called Grandmother's Buttons.

Owners Ellen and K. W. Kennon offer refreshments and encourage people to relax on the deck, lie in the hammock, or try the rope swing hanging from a backyard tree. Cool weather enticements might include warming by the fireplace or watching a football game. Hours are 10:00 A.M. to 5:00 P.M. Monday through Saturday and noon to 5:00 P.M. on Sunday. Call (504) 635–6116.

Afterward, continue to the **West Feliciana Historical Society Musuem** at 364 Ferdinand Street to pick up a map detailing a driving-walking tour of St. Francisville. While here take time to see the musuem's dioramas, displays of vintage clothing, documents, maps, and other interesting exhibits. The museum is open from 9:00 A.M. to 4:00 P.M. Monday through Saturday. Sunday hours are 1:00 to 4:00 P.M. The museum is free. Call (504) 635–6330. Afterward, a little backtracking down Ferdinand Street takes you to **Grace Episcopal Church,** one of the sites featured on your map.

This English Gothic-style church, surrounded by an old cemetery and a canopy of moss-covered oak trees, dates from 1858. The present brick structure replaces a smaller wooden church built on this site in 1828.

Stepping inside the church, you'll see divided pews, ornate plaster moldings, European and American stained glass, and an impressive bronze chandelier, which was once a gaslight. An organ, built and installed by the Henry Pilcher firm in 1860, is believed to be the oldest instrument of its type still in use.

During the Civil War when Grace Church received heavy damage from Yankee gunboats, an unusual incident occurred. The war stopped for the funeral of a Yankee gunboat commander in the churchyard cemetery as men in both blue and gray stood by. According to a published account, Union soldiers waving a white flag approached shore with the body of Lieutenant Commander John E. Hart. Hart had asked for a Masonic burial, and his fellow Confederate Masons honored the deathbed request. Behind Grace Church, you can see the marble monument with a Masonic emblem that marks Hart's grave.

Continue your tour of the town's historic district by returning to Royal Street and turning left. On your drive through a few clustered blocks, you'll see lovely houses, offices, banks, and churches.

Take a sightseeing break by stopping for lunch at the **Magnolia Cafe,** housed in a former gas station downtown at Commerce Street. The eatery features homemade pizzas, salads, sandwiches, and Mexican entrées. Try the turkey pita with Swiss cheese, guacamole, sprouts, and tomato or the muffuletta made with Italian bread, salami, ham, mozzarella, lettuce, and original olive oil mix. Prices are economical. Hours are Monday through Saturday from 10:00 A.M. to 4:00 P.M. Call (504) 635–6528.

Don't miss **The Myrtles,** an elegant home located on U.S. Highway 61, 1 mile north of Route 10. The plantation's name comes from the many crepe myrtles on the grounds. The oldest portion of the house was built around 1796 by General David Bradford, leader of the Whiskey Rebellion in Pennsylvania. Later

127

owners enlarged The Myrtles and added wide verandas trimmed in "iron lace," one of the house's trademarks. Inside, you'll see Italian marble mantels, mirrored doorknobs, and Irish and French crystal chandeliers. The house is also noted for its elaborate interior plasterwork—and its resident ghosts.

The mansion has been called one of America's most haunted houses. A local resident told me that she has never seen a ghost at The Myrtles, but she knows people who claim they have. One time when she and a group were performing the Virginia reel during a special event at The Myrtles, her dance partner suddenly asked, "Did you see them?" He then described two little girls, dressed in nightgowns, peering through a window. When he turned, they had vanished. Then there's the incident of the mirror allegedly hurled by a ghost at a former owner. Another story concerns a Confederate soldier who sat on a chair in the honeymooners' room. After lacing up his boots, he disappeared through the (closed) door.

Overnight accommodations feature beautifully furnished bedrooms and a delicious plantation breakfast. Rates are moderate. Except for major holidays the mansion is open for tours from 9:00 A.M. to 5:00 P.M. daily. Mystery tours are given at 8:30 P.M. on Friday and Saturday. Admission is charged. Call (504) 635–6277 for reservations.

Afterward, continue to ◆ **Butler Greenwood,** a plantation located 2.2 miles north of town on U.S. Highway 61. Watch for a sign on the left marking the tree-canopied drive that leads past a sunken garden and through a parklike setting. Before Hurricane Andrew blew in, says owner Anne Butler, one could not see sky through the arching live oaks—many of which grew from acorns brought from Haiti in 1799 by a planter's family.

A prolific writer whose published works span both fiction and nonfiction, Anne sandwiches in sentences between family responsibilities and guests. Her children Chase and Stewart make the eighth generation of the same family to live on this working plantation established during the 1790s.

On a tour of the English-style house, you'll see a formal Victorian parlor with a twelve-piece matched set of Louis XV rosewood furniture upholstered in its original red velvet. A Brussels carpet, French pier mirrors, and floor-to-ceiling windows topped by gilt cornices echo the room's elegance. Other treasures include a Prudent Mallard bed and dresser, oil portraits, and an extensive collection of vintage clothing.

Behind the main house (built before 1810) stands the plantation's original detached kitchen of slave-made brick, dating to 1796 when Spain ruled the region. Just beyond, overlooking a pond where deer come to drink, you'll see the cook's nineteenth-century cottage. Anne reserves these historical structures for overnight visitors, who get a tour of the main house, a continental breakfast, and a copy of her book, *A Tourist's Guide to West Feliciana Parish*. Rates are moderate. For reservations call 1–800–749–1928 or (504) 635–6312. Travelers also can sign up for bird and nature walks given by wildlife artist and naturalist Murrell Butler.

After leaving Butler Greenwood, continue north on U.S. Highway 61 to visit nearby **Catalpa**. Owner Mamie Fort Thompson, locally known as "Miss Mamie," gives delightful tours of her ancestral home that's "lived in, loved, and used." You'll see rosewood Mallard parlor pieces, a Pleyel piano, a Sèvres whale-oil lamp, crystal cranberry champagne glasses, antique china, porcelain, and silver. Miss Mamie shares personal anecdotes as she points out various pieces and paintings, such as the Thomas Sully portrait of her grandmother Sarah Turnbull from Rosedown. The home is filled with exceptional antiques but also brims over with the warmth and hospitality that come easily to a gracious hostess. Except for December and January, Catalpa is open for tours from 9:30 A.M. to 5:00 P.M. by appointment. Admission is charged. Call (504) 635–3372.

Afterward you may want to visit ◆ **The Cottage**, another interesting plantation home in the area. To reach The Cottage continue north on U.S. Highway 61. Watch for a turnoff sign on the right side of the road. Then follow the narrow lane that winds through the woods. You'll cross a small wooden bridge just before you reach the plantation complex.

Definitely off the beaten path, the main house is located in an idyllic setting, thick with trees draped in Spanish moss. If you have trouble locating The Cottage, you might be interested in knowing that Andrew Jackson found it when he and his officers stayed here on their way home after the Battle of New Orleans— without today's road signs.

The plantation house, a rambling two-story structure dating from 1795, features an inviting gallery with dormer windows above. On the long back porch, you're likely to see either Big Foot or Fat Cat curled up in a chair. The house still contains most of its original furniture—many of the same pieces that were here when General Jackson visited. Be sure to notice the unique turtle spittoon in the parlor and the set of servant bells with six different tones.

One of the state's oldest plantation complexes, The Cottage features a number of interesting outbuildings: the original detached kitchen, one-room school, milk house, smokehouse, tack room, barn, family cemetery, and slave cabins. In the carriage house you'll see a plush carriage with blue velvet upholstery and silver handles. According to a bill of sale on the wall, the carriage, which was bought by Thomas Butler in 1820, cost $1,000.

Except Christmas Day the home is open daily from 9:00 A.M. to 5:00 P.M. for tours. Admission is charged. The Cottage also offers bed and breakfast accommodations with prebreakfast coffee delivered to your room, a full plantation breakfast in the antique-filled dining room, and a house tour. Rates are moderate. For more information call (504) 635–3674.

Afterward, return to St. Francisville. At some point during your visit, stop by The Ramada Inn–St. Francis at the intersection of U.S. Highway 61 and State Route 10 to see the John J. Audubon gallery of prints on the premises. This exhibit features 435 original prints from a limited issue of the Amsterdam edition of *Birds of America.*

To learn more about Audubon, travel south on U.S. Highway 61 for a short distance, then turn left on Route 965. Continue 2.9 miles to reach **Oakley House,** the focal point of the **Audubon State Commemorative Area.** Noted naturalist John James Audubon worked here as a tutor while compiling his *Birds of America* series. Many first-edition Audubon prints line the walls at Oakley, which has been restored as a musuem to house Audubon memorabilia.

Each spring, St. Francisville hosts an **Audubon Pilgrimage** featuring plays, skits, and musicals. In these productions, performers dress in authentic costumes made from fabrics, patterns, and colors original to Audubon's period "right down to no zippers, elastic, or Velcro." The three-day pilgrimage features activities staged at Oakley as well as other area plantation homes and gardens.

After touring Oakley House, you can explore the formal gardens, nature trails, and wildlife sanctuary on the grounds. Except for Thanksgiving, Christmas Day, and New Year's Day, hours are 9:00 A.M. to 5:00 P.M. daily. Admission is modest. There's no charge for youngsters under thirteen or senior citizens; call (504) 635–3739.

After touring Oakley, follow Route 965 to ◆ **The Bluffs** on Thompson Creek and watch out for deer dashing across the road. You might call The Bluffs a bed and breakfast with a bonus— golf. Designed by Arnold Palmer, this championship course continues to collect accolades. *Golf Digest* recently rated it number two in the state. According to the project director Harold Leone, "If you build a great golf course, all other things come together." Taking advantage of a beautiful setting, the builders added thousands of azaleas and native dogwoods to enhance sweeping swaths of green punctuated by high bluffs. Advance tee times are required; call (504) 634–5551.

After your golf outing, enjoy lunch or dinner at the elegant **Clubhouse Restaurant** overlooking the golf course. You can opt for a casual meal in the grill or on the patio or enjoy the main dining room's Louisiana and European cuisine. I ordered the sensation salad followed by seafood in puff pastry with a rich brandy cream sauce—marvelous. If you go overboard on the Sunday buffet, served between 11:00 A.M. and 2:30 P.M., you can get matters back in hand with a round of golf. Prices are moderate. For reservations call (504) 634–5088. The Lodge at The Bluffs offers suites within walking distance of golf, tennis, pool, and restaurant. Rates are moderate. Call (504) 634–3410.

Afterward, return to St. Francisville and take State Route 10 east to complete your tour of "Louisiana's English Plantation Country" at Rosedown Plantation and Gardens.

◆ **Rosedown Plantation and Gardens** is located just east of St. Francisville on Route 10. This classic Greek Revival house was built in 1835 by a wealthy young couple, Martha and Daniel Turnbull, who patterned the plantation's thirty acres of lovely formal gardens after those they visited on their European honeymoon. They were especially inspired by the gardens at Versailles, and their avenues of shrubs and trees, formal parterres, and classical landscapes reflect a seventeenth-century French influence. You'll enjoy strolling through these magnificent gardens of winding paths bordered by camellias, azaleas, and ancient live oaks. Indigo, once valuable as a source of blue dye, grows at the base of a tree on the front lawn. Rosedown's gardens are especially delightful in spring. (Spring is an ideal time to visit Louisiana because the weather is pleasant then; autumn makes a good second choice.)

On certain excursions, passengers who board the *Delta Queen* or the *Mississippi Queen* in New Orleans can spend an afternoon exploring the mansion and grounds at Rosedown.

When you tour the home, you'll see some lovely period pieces; almost 90 percent of the original furniture is still here. The nursery, filled with family toys such as a wooden rocking horse and an antique doll in a high chair, is especially charming. In the music room, which contains some vintage instruments including a harp, you'll see a portrait that John James Audubon painted of his art student, Eliza Pirrie, during his stay at nearby Oakley House.

A custom-made mahogany Gothic bedroom suite, intended as a victory gift for Henry Clay, occupies Rosedown's north wing. When Clay lost the 1844 presidential election, Mr. Turnbull built a wing at Rosedown to hold the massive furniture (scaled for White House proportions). Then to balance the mansion's design, he added a library wing on the opposite end.

Except for Christmas Eve and Christmas Day, Rosedown is open daily. A house tour takes about forty-five minutes, but you'll need extra time for exploring the grounds. From March through October visiting hours are 9:00 A.M. to 5:00 P.M. The hours change to 10:00 A.M. until 4:00 P.M. from November through February. Admission is charged.

EAST FELICIANA PARISH

In Clinton, which became the parish seat in 1824, you'll see the **East Feliciana Parish Courthouse.** This stately Greek Revival structure, with twenty-eight columns and a domed, octagonal cupola atop a hipped roof, serves as the town's centerpiece. Be sure to walk around to the back of the courthouse, where you'll see a row of Greek Revival buildings that date from 1840 to 1860. These cottages, collectively known as Lawyers' Row, have also been designated a National Historic Landmark. Nearby Marston House, built in 1837 as a combination bank and house, may be visited by appointment. In April the East Feliciana Pilgrimage offers tours of the Marston House and other historic homes; call (504) 683–8677.

From Clinton take Route 10 east until you intersect Interstate 55. Travel south toward Hammond and then take the Springfield exit.

TANGIPAHOA PARISH

Near Hammond you can visit **Kliebert's Alligator Farm** (unless you're traveling during winter when alligators hibernate). Located at 1264 West Yellow Water Road, this unique facility is the world's largest working alligator farm. Jean and Harvey Kliebert, with the help of their son, Michael, and son-in-law, Bruce Mitchell, operate the reptile farm.

The Klieberts have been raising alligators for a long time. You'll probably see Big Fred, now 16 feet long, who was hatched here over three decades ago. The Klieberts' alligators surpass wild alligators in size because they're well fed. Feeding more than 5,000 alligators, a number of which measure from 9 to 14 feet long, requires plenty of food. The alligators eat chicken, nutria, fish, everything Harvey (who traps in winter) brings home, and "anything we can buy by the truckload," says Jean.

During June and July, you may observe a procedure called "taking the eggs," whereby two staff members, using long sticks, retrieve the alligators' eggs. Because these reptiles do not relish relinquishing their eggs, the collection process can prove quite challenging.

In addition to alligators, you'll see thousands of turtles as well as a bird rookery. During spring flocks of egrets and herons nest at the farm.

The Klieberts sell deboned alligator and turtle meat as well as alligator and turtle sausage. According to Jean, alligator sausage (which is mixed with pork) "tastes something like Italian sausage and is very good." Each year on the third Saturday in August, the Klieberts celebrate Annual Alligator Day with music and games and offer free food to visitors.

A guided walking tour of the farm takes from thirty to forty-five minutes. Except for the period from November 1 through March 1, the farm is open daily. Tours are offered from noon until 6:00 P.M. (or dark). Modest admission is charged. There's no charge for youngsters under two. Call (504) 345–3617.

After visiting the alligators, head southeast to nearby **Ponchatoula**—population 5,475. Already recognized as "Strawberry Capital of the World," the town flaunts a new title, "America's Antique City." Located at the junction of U.S. Highway 51 and Route 22, Ponchatoula takes its name from Choctaw Indian words for "hanging hair" (a reference to the ubiquitous Spanish moss dangling from area trees).

Ponchatoula's rebirth as an antique mecca happened in less than three years. "We went from twenty-four vacant downtown buildings to total occupancy," says local realtor and Main Street Program manager Charlene Daniels, one of the driving forces in the town's restoration. The transformation required a committed community effort plus plenty of paint, chosen from a palette of historical colors. Painters from Sheriff Charles Foti's Prison Art Program freshened up storefronts throughout the heart of town, a two-block National Historic District.

Well over 120 dealers offer their wares for shoppers who love poking among yesterday's treasures, antiques, crafts, bric-a-brac, and collectibles. Strolling along the sidewalk, you see changing still life compositions—a barber pole balanced against an antique pie safe, a rocking chair draped with a crazy quilt, or a hobbyhorse, doll, and vintage buggy.

Stop by the ✦ **Ponchatoula Country Market** in the heart of town. Housed in an 1854 historic depot, this bazaar offers booths of handcrafted items, antiques, collectibles, homemade jellies, and pastries. Beside the railroad station, you can visit the Mail Car Art Gallery, a restored baggage-mail car featuring the work of local artists. You may want to say hello to the town's mascot, "Old Hardhide." Not your average alligator, this one boasts his own bank account and local newspaper column (in which he espouses opinions that others dare not). He lives in a large wire cage in front of the railroad station.

Across the street, you'll find the Collinswood School Museum. This old-fashioned schoolhouse, which dates from around 1876, contains artifacts and memorabilia pertaining to the area's history. Next door at 123 West Pine Street, **Layrisson Walker LTD** features antique linens, hats, rugs, quilts, jewelry, books, and vintage clothing and furnishings. Shop hours run Wednesday through Saturday from 10:00 A.M. to 5:00 P.M. and from 1:00 to 5:00 P.M. on Sunday. Call (504) 386–8759.

Afterward, take an old-fashioned nectar soda break at **Cafe CJ** at 129 East Pine in the Old Southern Gateway Hotel. You can also fortify yourself with a salad, sandwich, soup, or dessert. At 195 East Pine, Karen Travelbee's **Terra Cotta Plus** features handcrafted Monterrey pottery, terra cotta patio fireplaces, unique table bases, and garden accessories.

Cross the street to browse through **Ponchatoula Feed and Seed,** an old-fashioned store that carries farm and garden supplies, baby chicks, hardware, and bedding plants. Continue your exploration down the block and across railroad tracks.

Don't miss **Zotti,** an antique shop at 116 West Pine on the corner across from the tourist information booth. Owner Victor Zotti features furniture, decorative accessories, books, and collectibles. Hours are Wednesday through Saturday from 10:00 A.M. to 5:00 P.M. and from noon to 5:00 P.M. on Sunday. Call (504) 386–6414. By the way, Victor welcomes bed and breakfast guests to **Eleven Pecans Country House,** his circa 1860 cypress Acadian cottage in nearby Springfield. The home's exterior features natural wooded landscaping, bright striped canopies, and twin stone lions standing guard by the door. "Breakfast is wonderful," promises Victor, who serves guests on the deck. He often prepares grits and *grillades,* a marvelous Creole breakfast specialty of veal medallions in a reddish-brown spicy sauce, poured over hot grits and accompanied by homemade biscuits. For reservations, call (504) 695–3344.

While continuing your exploration in downtown Ponchatoula, stop for lunch or dinner at Patricia Lambert's **C'est Bon,** a restaurant at 131 Southwest Railroad Avenue. Try an appetizer of eggplant C'est Bon followed by the bourbon pecan chicken—scrumptious. Prices are moderate. Call (504) 386–4077.

Except for a spirited Saturday night antique auction, town hours generally run from 10:00 A.M. to 5:00 P.M. Monday through Saturday and from 11:00 A.M. to 5:00 P.M. on Sunday. (About half the shops close on Monday, and a few close on Tuesday.)

On your way out, stop by **Taste of Bavaria,** a bakery and restaurant on the town's western outskirts. You can pick up some great German breads and pastries to go or enjoy a meal on the premises.

135

ST. TAMMANY PARISH

From Ponchatoula take Route 22 east to Madisonville, a charming little town on the northern shore of Lake Pontchartrain. You can make your base at ◆ **River Run Bed and Breakfast** on the Tchefuncta (cha-FUNK-ta) River. Liz and Richard Kempe and their two daughters moved to this century-old house, located at 703 Main Street, from New Orleans. Prior to that the Kempes served in the Peace Corps and lived in the Seychelles (south of the equator in the middle of the Indian Ocean).

They have renovated three upstairs bedrooms and a large bathroom, which guests share. Richard, a contract estimator, handles the construction and electrical work, and Liz does the painting.

The Kempes will let you borrow a canoe or a bike to take in the local sites. River Run also makes a convenient place to headquarter while visiting New Orleans. Taking the nearby Lake Pontchartrain Causeway, a 24-mile bridge connecting St. Tammany Parish to New Orleans, you can arrive in the heart of the city in about forty-five minutes. Some guests who come for Mardi Gras festivities make daily trips from Madisonville.

Liz takes coffee up to her guests and taps on their doors to wake them at requested times. She serves a healthy breakfast, which may consist of juice, fruit salad, yogurt, multigrain waffles, and plenty of good South Louisiana coffee. When I visited in mid-December, Liz and I enjoyed a pleasant outdoor breakfast on the front porch, festive with Christmas decorations. "We cater to couples who are looking for quiet surroundings and affordable accommodations," she says. Rates are standard. Call (504) 845–4222.

A few steps down the street from River Run, you'll find **Madison Cottage Antiques.** Located at 707 Main Street on the corner of routes 22 and 21, this shop is owned by Karen Sadowski and Pam Simmers. Besides antiques they carry an array of gift items, mirrors, English china, collectibles, and not-to-be-missed hot pepper jelly (Karen's jelly won first place at the St. Tammany Parish Fair). Watercolorist Dottie Moore exhibits her work here, and the complex also houses jewelry and needlepoint shops. For more information call (504) 845–4706. After shopping, take a break at **Annex Coffee** located behind Madison Antiques, where owners Robert and James Simmers feature gourmet coffees, desserts, and daiquiris. The coffee shop is open from 8:00 A.M. to 5:00 P.M. weekdays and until 8:00 P.M. on weekends. Call (504) 845–9494.

For dinner you can visit **Friends on the Tchefuncta,** located at 407 St. Tammany. The seafood is scrumptious, and you can look out over the Tchefuncta River as you dine. If you're in the mood, you can start with a cool and creamy drink, appropriately called Blue Bayou.

An order of grilled shrimp and scallops wrapped in bacon makes a good appetizer. For an entrée consider grilled amberjack, served with California sweet onions and herb butter or perhaps soft-shell crab with slivered almonds. Death by Chocolate, a rich cake made with five kinds of chocolate and topped with chocolate bits, may be on the dessert menu. It's reputed to be delicious, and since I didn't step over any bodies on my way out, I assume it's not entirely lethal.

The restaurant opens at 11 A.M. Tuesday through Sunday. Seatings are taken until 9:00 P.M. on weeknights and until 10:00 P.M. on weekends. For reservations call (504) 845–7303.

Two miles east of Madisonville on Route 22, you'll find Fairview-Riverside State Park, which offers great fishing, camping, and picnicking. Continuing on to Mandeville, almost within shouting distance, be sure to drive along the town's lovely lakefront. Lakeshore Restaurant, located at 2221 Lakeshore Drive, offers some delicious luncheon and dinner specials.

A short distance southeast of Mandeville, you'll discover Fontainebleau State Park, which covers 2,700 acres on the shores of Lake Pontchartrain. The park features the brick ruins of an old sugar mill, covered picnic pavilions, and nature trails.

Before leaving the area make a short excursion north to Covington. In the town's historic district, you may want to stop by some of the **Lee Lane Shops.** These Creole cottages, dating from the nineteenth century, have been converted to specialty shops, which carry antiques, art, gifts, clothing, and other items.

Don't miss **H. J. Smith's Son General Store,** located at 308 North Columbia Street in downtown Covington. This old-time country store, which also features a museum, sells everything from ox yokes and cast-iron stoves to plantation bells. On the front porch you'll see a buckboard and an inviting swing. Other merchandise consists of cypress swings, oak rockers, wood-burning stoves, and various hardware and farm supplies. Inside the store a corn crib more than 150 years old serves as a display area for kerosene lamps, crockery, and cast-iron cookware.

The museum contains hundreds of items from yesteryear, such as an old metal ice box, a century-old cypress dugout boat, and a cast-iron casket. A hand-operated wooden washing machine, old cotton scales, and various vintage tools are also on display. Call (504) 892–0460.

St. Tammany Parish boasts the country's largest llama breeding ranch and a number of thoroughbred horse farms. But the area's most remote and mysterious spot, as far as getting off the beaten path goes, is Honey Island Swamp on the eastern edge of the parish between Louisiana and Mississippi.

To reach Honey Island Swamp, head toward Slidell in the state's southeastern corner. A good way to explore this pristine wilderness is to take one of ◆ **Dr. Wagner's Honey Island Swamp Tours.** Tours depart from Crawford Landing, about 5 miles east of Slidell on the West Pearl River. Dr. Paul Wagner is a wetlands ecologist, and he or one of his staff will introduce you to this wild 250-square-mile region.

Because it attracted large swarms of honeybees, early settlers called the place Honey Island. One of America's least explored swamps, this area is home to a large variety of plants and wildlife—and maybe even the mysterious swamp monster, Wookie. Some hunters and fishermen swear that they've seen the creature, which they consistently describe as about 7 feet tall and covered with short hair, longer at the scalp. Wookie supposedly walks upright and leaves four-toed tracks. So far nobody on the tours has spotted said creature, but if it exists, then this wild and dense area seems an appropriate environment.

Although you may miss Wookie, you'll see some of the swamp's resident and migratory birds: herons, ibis, egrets, bald eagles, owls, and wild turkeys. Crawfish, turtles, alligators, wild boar, deer, and otter also live here.

The Wagners serve as stewards of the Louisiana Nature Conservancy's White River Tract, and the tour includes a visit to this beautiful area, teeming with wildlife. This "microcosm of a swamp," as Dr. Wagner puts it, contains a rookery, a wood duck roost, and an active bald eagle nest where generations of eagles have come for some fifty years.

A number of visitors return to see the swamp's seasonal changes. In spring and summer, the place becomes lush like a rain forest, but cool weather months offer improved visibility. Tours leave at 9:00 A.M. and 2:00 P.M. (4:00 P.M. during the summer), and reservations are required. A typical tour takes about two hours. Admission is charged. The Wagners also offer a hotel pickup service from New Orleans—complete with a narrated tour of the city. Credit cards are not accepted. Call the Wagners at (504) 641–1769.

After leaving Honey Island, you will be on the threshold of New Orleans (N'yawlins). Major tourist mecca that it is, New Orleans cannot be considered off the beaten path; however, it offers some unique sites and cityscapes that you may want to include on your itinerary. If so, take nearby Interstate 10 and cross the twin-span bridge over the end of Lake Pontchartrain into America's Paris.

ORLEANS PARISH

New Orleans, famous for its food, music, festivals, architecture, history, and carefree atmosphere, is a city like no other. New Orleans has been described as magical, rambunctious, debonair, flamboyant, seductive, and yes, decadent—but most of all, it's fascinating.

The city hosts a number of festivals. Carnival season starts on January 6, and the excitement continues to mount until Mardi Gras, the last two weeks of Carnival. Other events include the Spring Fiesta and the Tennessee Williams/New Orleans Literary Festival, also held during spring. Music buffs will enjoy the annual New Orleans Jazz and Heritage Festival, featuring thousands of musicians in a series of performances. This gala is usually staged from the last weekend of April through the first weekend in May. Spring is an ideal time to visit New Orleans—it's no secret that summer days can fall in the sweaty and sweltering category.

Before beginning your exploration of the Crescent City (so called because of its location on a large crescent of the Mississippi River), throw away your compass. New Orleans' confusing geography takes a while to master. Natives refer to uptown as south and downtown as north; the two other major directions are lake-side (toward Lake Pontchartrain) and riverside. You can get a good view of the crescent from Moonwalk, a promenade that fronts the French Quarter and overlooks the Mississippi River. *A word of warning:* As you explore New Orleans, it's best to stick to the beaten path, avoiding any questionable areas. New Orleans can appear deceptively safe, so don't forget to exercise the same caution that you would in any major city.

If New Orleans is your exclusive destination, consider coming by plane or train. An Amtrak excursion with sleeping car, which includes meals and other amenities, will allow you to arrive rested and ready to tackle The Big Easy. For reservations and information call 1–800–USA–RAIL. In this city of precious parking (not to mention the French Quarter's narrow streets), a car has definite drawbacks. United Cabs offer reliable and courteous service; call (504) 522–9771 or (504) 524–9606. Also, the St. Charles Streetcar, listed on the National Register of Historic Places, affords an entertaining and inexpensive way to get about. You may want to purchase a pass for a day of unlimited rides.

For comfort and convenience with some marbled opulence thrown in for good measure, plan to stay at ◆ **Le Pavillon Hotel.** Fronted by large columns and ornamented with sculptures and cast terra cotta garlands, Le Pavillon stands at 833 Poydras Street on the corner of Baronne. A member of Historic Hotels of America, this 1907 architectural classic offers spacious rooms and suites along with friendly service. The lobby's crystal chandeliers came from Czechoslovakia and its marble railings from the Grand Hotel in Paris. Each of the hotel's seven deluxe suites features a different decor. From antique to art deco, all furnishings, paintings, and accents carry out the room's theme.

Guests can take a dip in the rooftop pool and relax on the patio with its sweeping view of the Mississippi River. After a night on the town, stop by the lobby for a complimentary late-night snack of peanut butter and jelly sandwiches (made with home-made bread) with a glass of milk. Rates are moderate to deluxe. For reservations call 1–800–535–9095 or (504) 581–3111.

After settling in, start your sightseeing session in the nearby French Quarter with beignets and *cafe au lait* at **Cafe du Monde**. Afterward, stroll through the Vieux Carre (view-ka-ray), as the old French Quarter also is known. Save some time to watch the street performers in Jackson Square with its famous artists' fence. Clopping through the Quarter, straw-hatted mules pull surreys and carriages—a relaxing way to see the stately tri-towered St. Louis Cathedral, outdoor cafes, and "frozen lace" galleries.

For lunch or dinner, stop by the ◆ **G & E Courtyard Grill** at 1113 Decatur Street. Chef/proprietor Michael Uddo named the restaurant in honor of his grandparents, Giuseppe and Eleanora, who sailed to New Orleans from Sicily in 1907. They settled on lower Decatur Street, then called Little Italy, and worked hard in food-related ventures. Success followed. Their portraits hang in the restaurant, a reminder of Michael's legacy. His philosophy, stated on the menu, reads: "Freshness and simplicity are not just common terms used to describe great cooking. They are goals chefs work a lifetime to reach."

You can enjoy that freshness and simplicity while savoring seafood pasta in the courtyard with its garden where Michael grows herbs organically to enhance his menu offerings. Consider starting with an appetizer of wild mushrooms under glass in a light madeira cream or a wilted spinach salad with smoked bacon. For an entrée, order the sautéed freshwater striped bass or perhaps fresh roasted eggplant and prosciutto with penne pasta. Lunch hours run from 11:00 A.M. to 3:00 P.M. Tuesday through Sunday (till midnight on Friday and Saturday). Call (504) 528–9376.

While in the French Quarter with its many enticements, consider touring the **Beauregard-Keyes House** at 1113 Chartres Street just across from the Old Ursuline Convent. Frances Parkinson Keyes (kize), author of fifty-one books, lived here while writing *Dinner at Antoine's, Blue Camellia,* and other novels. Docents, dressed in period costume, give guided tours Monday through Saturday, from 10:00 A.M. to 3:00 P.M. The gift shop offers a wide selection of the author's books. Admission is modest. Call (504) 523–7257.

Stop by the **New Orleans Pharmacy Museum,** also known as La Pharmacie Française at 514 Rue Chartres. The bay windows feature some colorful eye-catching decanters called show globes. These jars stack on top of one another (each serves as a stopper for the one below) and are filled with red, green, and blue liquids "symbolic of the mystery and secrecy of medicine and drugs," says museum director Clara Bakar.

Entering the museum you have the sense of stepping into a nineteenth-century apothecary shop. You'll see shelves lined with hand-blown antique apothecary jars, patent medicines, placebos, medicinal herbs, and *gris-gris* potions used in the practice of voodoo. Many of the old medicine bottles are still filled with their original contents—except for the jars that held leeches (once used to treat high blood pressure through bloodletting). Be sure to notice the collection of Civil War surgical instruments, the Belgian slate floors, and the beautiful 1850 soda fountain made of black and rose marble.

The shop occupies the first floor of a Creole-American townhouse, built in 1823 for Louis J. Dufilho, Jr., America's first licensed pharmacist. Behind the museum there's a lovely walled courtyard with an herb garden. You can also browse among the exhibits upstairs. Brochures are available on such topics as the medicinal uses of garlic and medical practices of the nineteenth century. The museum is open from 10:00 A.M. to 5:00 P.M. Tuesday through Sunday and closes on Monday. A nominal donation is requested. Call (504) 524–9077.

Afterward, take a break at nearby **Napoleon House.** This interesting old building at 500 Chartres Street houses a bar and cafe. You can study the menu, printed on fans with faces of Napoleon and Josephine, while listening to classical music in the background. Try the house specialty, an Italian muffuletta, a great sandwich with meats, cheeses, and olive salad.

After browsing through the Quarter's antique shops, art galleries, and boutiques, consider taking a stroll along Riverwalk and visiting **Aquarium of the Americas**, where you can get nose to nose with a shark, see white alligators, and hold a parrot in the Amazon rain forest. Also, you might like to buy a copy of *New Orleans for Kids,* an activity book and tour guide available at the Greater New Orleans Tourist and Convention Commission at 1520 Sugar Bowl Drive. Speaking of books, consider picking up *The New Orleans Eat Book* by native Tom Fitzmorris, who gives you an entertaining, tried and true rundown of three hundred of the city's great eateries. You could make a career out of trying New Orleans restaurants.

Afterward, head for Canal Street, a few blocks away. This wide avenue divides the French Quarter from "American territory" in uptown New Orleans. On Canal you can catch the St. Charles

Streetcar—one rattles by every ten minutes—for a ride through the **Garden District**. Bumping along you'll see handsome nineteenth-century villas, Greek Revival mansions, and raised cottages surrounded by magnolias and ancient live oaks. This lovely area, with its lush landscaping and extravagant gardens dotted with statuary and fountains, makes a fine place to stroll. By walking you can better admire the ornamental iron fences with their geometric and plant motifs.

Even better, sign up for a Garden District tour by a ranger from the French Quarter Unit of Jean Lafitte National Historic Park and Preserve. The Faubourg Promenade starts at 2:30 P.M. from the corner of First Street and St. Charles Avenue in the Garden District. The tour takes about ninety minutes, so wear your walking shoes. Except for Christmas Day and Mardi Gras, the tours take place daily and are free. Reservations are required. Call (504) 589–2636.

⬧**The Sully Mansion** at 2631 Prytania Street on the corner of Fourth Street opens its lovely front door to guests who want to headquarter in the heart of Garden District. This rare and charming Queen Anne Victorian circa 1890 design by New Orleans architect Thomas Sully "is one of the most intact of the few remaining Sullys in the city," says owner Maralee Prigmore. Eclectically furnished, the high-ceilinged home features ten-foot cypress doors, a grand staircase, original stained glass, ornate ceiling medallions, and heart-of-pine floors.

Maralee maintains shelves of old magazines upstairs, which guests love to look through. She serves a continental breakfast of fresh fruit, cereal, croissants, and coffee. Rates are standard to moderate. Call (504) 891–0457.

Nearby, you can catch the St. Charles Streetcar for more sightseeing or take a short stroll to **Commander's Palace,** one of the city's many wonderful restaurants. Housed in a Victorian mansion at 1403 Washington Avenue, the famous eatery features spectacular Creole cuisine and superb seafood. Start with a Commander's specialty, tasty turtle soup. For an entrée, you might order roasted Louisiana quail filled with shrimp and crabmeat, roast rack of lamb, or tournedos done to your taste. Don't skip dessert here. (You can walk it off later.) Try Commander's Creole bread pudding soufflé or the flamed and famed celebration dessert starring raspberries and chocolate.

Except for Mardi Gras, Christmas Eve, and Christmas Day, Commander's Palace is open from 11:00 A.M. to 2:00 P.M. and 6:00 to 10:00 P.M. Monday through Friday. On weekends you can enjoy a Dixieland jazz brunch. Saturday hours are 11:30 A.M. to 2:00 P.M.; Sunday brunch begins at 10:30 A.M. Prices are expensive. For reservations call (504) 899–8221.

For another delightful place to hang your hat in this area, head to **The Josephine** located just at the edge of the Garden District. Owned by Mary Ann Weilbaecher and husband Dan Fuselier, this guest house stands at 1450 Josephine Street on the corner of Prytania. The Italianate-style home dates to 1870 and houses such striking antiques as "the jewel of the Josephine," an ornate ebony bed with inlaid ivory designs of dancing nymphs. The bed, which Dan calls "a bit on the risqué side," was recently featured in a bridal magazine.

Mary Ann, who studied cookery in Paris, makes fresh breads, which she serves with juice and *cafe au lait* on Wedgwood china and presents on a silver tray. The couple offers recommendations and makes reservations for guests. "We like to help dock our guests," says Dan. Rates are moderate. For reservations call 1–800–779–6361 or (504) 524–6361.

On St. Charles Avenue you may want to visit ◆**Audubon Park** in a pretty setting with ancient live oaks, flower-filled gardens, and wandering lagoons. The 400-acre urban park also offers a golf course, tennis courts, and picnic facilities as well as walking and jogging paths. At Cascade Stables in the park, you can rent a horse and go galloping off along a tree-shaded trail that offers glimpses of St. Charles Avenue.

A free shuttle transports visitors from the streetcar line to nearby Audubon Zoo. Noted for its simulated barrier-free natural habitats, the zoo also makes a delightful outing, complete with peanuts, popcorn, and more than a thousand animals.

Afterward, you can either walk back to St. Charles for the streetcar or catch the bus on **Magazine Street**. Located in 2855 Magazine Street, Accent Antiques, owned by Patrick Richie, features a large selection of American and European period pieces as well as china, crystal, and unique items such as an oak glove case. At 3123 Magazine Street you'll find Collector Antiques. This shop offers antique linens, quilts, porcelain, picture frames, inkwells, and antique gifts. At 5415 Magazine Street you can browse for gifts through Libby Bonner's shop, British Antiques.

You'll come across some excellent buys in both English and French antiques along Magazine Street's 6 miles of shops, arcades, and galleries filled with furniture, paintings, china, crystal, silver, collectibles, and souvenirs. You'll also pass brass dealers, bookstores, restaurants, and specialty shops. Even though most of the stores don't have fancy façades (some even resemble junk shops), you can find some quality merchandise at bargain prices.

For a delectable dinner, try ◆ **Gautreau's,** a small uptown restaurant at 1728 Soniat Street. Four blocks from St. Charles Avenue, the eatery occupies a former neighborhood drugstore. Notice the antique pharmacy cases, reincarnated as wine cabinets, and the ceiling of embossed tin. A previous owner and descendant of Mme. Pierre Gautreau, the subject of John Singer Sargent's *Portrait of Madame X,* named the restaurant in honor of this celebrated beauty of nineteenth-century Paris. A reproduction of the Sargent portrait hangs on one of the restaurant's burgundy-colored walls.

Enough about decor. Chef Larkin Selman (also an owner) brings his particular panache to food preparation and presentation at this revised edition of Gautreau's, already known for its fine food and excellent service. You might start with an appetizer of crab cakes, enhanced by a spicy cilantro sauce. As for entrées, try one of the fish dishes such as sautéed tilapia, presented on marinated white beans with artichokes, arugula, and tarragon, or the grilled salmon with equally original accompaniments. Beef lovers won't be disappointed, either, because the restaurant serves a fine filet mignon with creative side dishes. For dessert, let yourself go and indulge in the *crème brulée* with sauce of triple sec, orange zest, and brown sugar. Hours are Monday through Saturday from 6:00 to 10:00 P.M. Prices are moderate to expensive. For reservations call (504) 899–7397.

At some point during your visit, schedule a boat ride to experience the mighty Mississippi's romance and majesty. Describing the Mississippi, Mark Twain called it "not a commonplace river, but in all ways remarkable." For a taste of Mr. Twain's river, you can choose a short ferry trip or a longer excursion on the *Creole Queen,* the *Natchez,* or another of the local

145

riverboats. Some cruises combine sightseeing with jazz, dinner, or Sunday brunch.

For a real taste of the river, grab your bag and head for the ◆ **Delta Queen Steamboat Company,** located at 30 Robin Street Wharf about two blocks from the Convention Center. Here you can set off on an overnight luxury cruise from New Orleans aboard the ***Delta Queen*** or the ***Mississippi Queen.*** Better yet, start or end your steamboat journey at the **Maison Dupuy** in the French Quarter. Located at 1001 Toulouse Street, this hotel (owned and operated by the Delta Queen Steamboat Company) offers a choice of accommodations from rooms to VIP suites. Best of all, you simply set your tagged bags outside your room on departure morning, and they magically reappear in your steamboat stateroom the same afternoon. Call (504) 586–8000 or 1–800–535–9177.

Steamboatin' on the Mississippi affords a pleasant way to forsake the beaten path as you leisurely roll up the river in a floating first-class hotel. At certain river ports you can get off the boat and tour plantation homes such as Houmas House, Nottoway, or Rosedown. Although your cruise can start and end in New Orleans, the big stern-wheelers also travel to other cities such as Memphis, St. Louis, Cincinnati, Pittsburgh, and St. Paul.

A "riverlorian" acquaints landlubbers with nautical terms so they can distinguish between port and starboard, understand mile markers, and identify the contents of passing barges. (Take your binoculars.) Adding to the ambience, the mighty steam calliope pumps out tunes like "Cruising Down the River," and "In the Good Old Summertime." Passengers get a turn at the great iron piano, too, and may take home a "Vox Calliopus" certificate, signed by the captain. Steamboatin' diversions range from sing-alongs and kite-flying over the big red paddlewheel to nightly steamboat-style entertainment, ballroom dancing, and big band sounds. And ah, the food—the traditional three meals plus afternoon tea and a midnight buffet, all superb and splendidly presented.

Excursions range from two to twelve nights. Rates based on double occupancy vary depending on boat and cabin size. The price includes all onboard meals and entertainment. Rates are deluxe. For more information, write to the Delta Queen Steamboat Company, Number 30 Robin Street Wharf, PXR1, New Orleans, LA 70130, or call 1–800–543–1949.

The *Delta Queen*

Finally, New Orleans can serve as a springboard for an outing to the ◆ **Chandeleur Islands**. It's difficult to get *more* off the beaten path than here on the barrier islands off Louisiana's eastern Gulf Coast; in fact, there's not even a path. There are no roads or hotels, either. "They're in the middle of no place and very pretty," says Steve Littleton, who transports visitors to the islands via float plane from New Orleans. It takes about thirty minutes to reach the beaches of this 50-mile-long barrier island chain, located some 25 miles from the mainland.

"The place is a bird sanctuary," Steve says, "and it's barren for miles and miles with lots of sand beaches." Every spring terns from around the Gulf of Mexico congregate in colossal numbers to breed on the Chandeleurs. You can see hundreds of thousands of birds including royal terns, sandwich terns, least terns, Forster's terns, laughing gulls, and black skimmers, which fly here for their annual family reunion during April, May, and June.

If you want to visit the Chandeleurs, either for birding or fishing (which is also terrific), Steve will deliver and collect you at a specified time or serve as guide. Steve lands in the water and taxis up to the beach, using his plane as a base of operations.

The Breton National Wildlife Refuge will allow you to camp on the Chandeleur Islands for up to a week if you promise not to bother the birds, which translates to keeping a distance of 200 yards away from the bird colonies.

Steve, who provides ice and soft drinks, will bring lunch if you request, or you can pack your own. The rate runs $400 for a round trip party of three; credit cards are not accepted. Steve meets his passengers in east New Orleans at the Lake Front Airport. For more information, you can call Steve at Trans-Gulf Seaplane Service; the number is (504) 254–0621.

INDEX

149